|| śrī-gaura-haraye namaḥ ||

मूलरामायणम्

Mūla-rāmāyaṇa

The Original Rāmāyaṇa

As narrated by Nārada Muni to Vālmīki

Second Edition, 2022

English and Hindi translation, Sanskrit prose order, word-for-word meaning and grammatical analysis

by

Demian Martins (Ph.D.)

Cover: *Śrī-Śrī-Sītā-Rāma, Lakṣmaṇa and Hanumān, the presiding deities of the Palimaru Maṭha, Udupi, installed by Śrī Madhvācārya (1238-1317).*

Preface

Once upon a time, while the sage Vālmīki was performing austerities on the bank of the river Tamasā, Nārada Muni appeared before him and narrated a summary of the *Rāmāyaṇa*, called the "*Mūla-rāmāyaṇa*" or the *Original Rāmāyaṇa*. This is the very first chapter in the *Bāla-kāṇḍa* of Vālmīki's *Rāmāyaṇa* and it consists of the main episodes of Śrī Rāma's pastimes summarized in one hundred verses. The text[1] itself suggests that the meeting of the sages took place some time after Śrī Rāma had defeated Rāvaṇa and before He became the king of Ayodhyā. After hearing the *Mūla-rāmāyaṇa*, the sage Vālmīki composed thousands of Sanskrit verses to elaborately narrate all the incidents in this great epic. Accepted as avatars of Lord Viṣṇu and Lord Śiva respectively, Śrī Rāma and Hanumān are some of the most beloved among the divinities in Hinduism and are worshipped in thousands of temples all over the world. For many centuries, Vālmīki has been known as the *ādi-kavi*, the first poet, and his *Rāmāyaṇa* is considered by many as the most ancient poem, so famous in the Indian subcontinent that its story line is known in nearly every house. After the *Mahābhārata*, Vālmīki's *Rāmāyaṇa* is the second greatest Sanskrit epic and it has influenced the philosophy, religion and culture of India for centuries. It remarkably influenced the later Sanskrit poetry, drama and

---

[1] See text 92.

literature, and inspired many poets to write their own versions of the epic, among which some of the most notable are Kālidāsa's Sanskrit *mahākāvya* "*Raghu-vaṁśa,*" written in the 5th century C.E., and Tulasīdāsa's "*Rāma-carita-mānasa,*" written in *Avadhī* in the 16th century, which became so popular in North India.

Although in its present form the whole *Vālmīki Rāmāyaṇa* text contains approximately twenty four thousand verses, many scholars hold the view that a good number of these were interpolated. Some even consider the whole *Uttara-kāṇḍa* a later addition not written by Vālmīki. There are indeed substantial differences between the several recensions of the *Vālmīki Rāmāyaṇa*, and even the *Mūla-rāmāyaṇa* appears with a different number of verses in different editions. Despite these discrepancies, the *Vālmīki Rāmāyaṇa* maintains its status as a sacred scripture and is venerated by millions.

As the "*Mūla-rāmāyaṇa*" has been used as a text book in innumerable colleges and schools all over India, I prepared this bilingual translation intending to fulfil the needs of a broad range of students. The grammatical analysis here is not meant to be exhaustive but to present the basic morphological classification of the vocabulary and some elements of the syntax. The word-for-word meaning was done with the help of three traditional Sanskrit commentaries: Govindarāja's *Rāmāyaṇa-bhūṣaṇa*, Nāgojī Bhaṭṭa's *Rāmāyaṇa-tilaka* and Śiva-sahāya's *Rāmāyaṇa-śiromaṇi.* The prose order (*anvaya*) of the Sanskrit texts was done according to the way the verses were interpreted and translated, but readers should bear in mind that there are other possible variations. For didactic purposes, the English and Hindi translations are mostly literal. Yet, to avoid compromising the natural flow of the language, some grammatical permutations are also found. For instance, some sentences that in the original text are in the passive voice, so common in Sanskrit, were translated in the active voice in English. The names of the seven *kāṇḍas* (sections) are not in the original but were added here for easy reference.

Acknowledgements

I would like to thank Mahāprabhu Dāsa, Jānakī-rāma Dāsa (Dr. Jonathan Edelmann) and Prema-sindhu Gaurāṅga Dāsa for helping to revise the text and for their valuable suggestions. I am also obliged to Vraja-ramaṇa Dāsa, who tirelessly did the final proofreading and made the text as flawless as possible.

Dr. Demian Martins

Vṛndāvana, 18th August, 2014

Śrī Kṛṣṇa Janmāṣṭamī

Abbreviations

abs.– absolutive (gerund), पूर्वकालिक कृदन्त
app.– active past participle, भूतकालिक कृदन्त
acc.– accusative case, द्वितीया विभक्ति
adj.– adjective, विशेषण
aff.– affix, प्रत्यय
aor.– aorist, लुङ् / भूतकाल
bv. cp.– bahuvrīhi compound, बहुव्रीहि समास
d. pron.– demonstrative pronoun, निश्चयवाचक सर्वनाम
dva. cp.– dual compound, द्वंद्व समास
f.– feminine, स्त्रीलिंग
fut.– future tense, लृट् / सामान्य भविष्यत् काल
gen.- genitive case, षष्ठी विभक्ति
imp.– imperfect tense, लङ् / सामान्य भूतकाल
indef. pron.– indefinite pronoun, अनिश्चयवाचक सर्वनाम
ipt.– imperative, लोट् / विधिकाल
ind.– indeclinable, अव्यय
inf.– infinitive, सामान्य क्रिया
inst.– instrumental case, तृतीया विभक्ति
int. pron.– interrogative pronoun, प्रश्नवाचक सर्वनाम
loc.– locative case, सप्तमी विभक्ति
loc. abs.– locative absolute, उपपद सप्तमी
m.– masculine, पुंल्लिंग
n.– noun, संज्ञा
neu.– neuter, नपुंसक लिंग
nom.– nominative case, प्रथमा विभक्ति

num.– numeral, संख्या
p.– person, पुरुष
ps.– passive, कर्मवाच्य
perf.– perfect tense, लिट् / पूर्ण भूतकाल
pl.– plural, बहुवचन
ppp.– past passive participle, भूतकालिक कर्मवाचक कृदन्त
p. pron.– personal pronoun, व्यक्तिवाचक सर्वनाम
pr.– present tense, लट् / सामान्य वर्तमान काल
pref.– prefix, उपसर्ग
prp.– present participle, वर्तमान कालिक कृदन्त
pr.pp.– present passive participle, वर्तमान कर्मवाचक कृदन्त
pron. adj.– pronominal adjective, विशेषण
r. pron.– relative pronoun, संबंधवाचक सर्वनाम
sg.– singular, एकवचन
tp. cp.– tatpuruṣa compound, तत्पुरुष समास
voc.– vocative, संबोधन

Bāla-kāṇḍa

TEXT 1

तपःस्वाध्यायनिरतं तपस्वी वाग्विदां वरम् ।
नारदं परिपप्रच्छ वाल्मीकिर्मुनिपुङ्गवम् ॥ १ ॥

tapaḥ-svādhyāya-nirataṁ tapasvī vāg-vidāṁ varam |

nāradaṁ paripapraccha vālmīkir muni-puṅgavam || 1 ||

tapaḥ– (neu. n.) austerity; **svādhyāya**– (m. n.) study of the Vedas; **nirata**– (ppp./adj.[1]) constantly engaged; **tapaḥ-svādhyāya-niratam**– (tp. cp./m. adj. acc. sg.) engaged in austerities and study of the Vedic scriptures; **tapasvī**– (m. n. nom. sg.) ascetic; **vāk**– (f.n.) speech, the words of the Vedas; **vid**– (adj.) knower; **vāg-vidām**– (tp. cp./m. n. gen. pl.) of those expert in speech or the words of the Vedas; **varam**– (m. adj. acc. sg.) the best; **nāradam**– (m. n. acc. sg.) the sage called Nārada[2]; **paripapraccha**– (pari + √ prach, perf. 3rd p. sg.) enquired;

---

[1] Words such as *nirata* (from ni + √ ram) are morphologically past passive particles but are also used as adjectives.

[2] The dictionary *Śabda-kalpa-druma* defines the name *Nārada* as *nāraṁ paramātma-viṣayakaṁ jñānaṁ dadātīti:* a person who gives knowledge about the Supreme Soul. Nārada Muni was born from the mind of Lord Brahmā. He appears frequently in the epics, *Purāṇas* and *Tantras.*

vālmīkiḥ– (m. n. nom. sg.) the sage called Vālmīki[3]; **muni**– (m. n.) sage; **puṅgava**– (adj.) the most exalted; **muni-puṅgavam**– (tp. cp./m. adj. acc. sg.) the most exalted of sages.

Prose order *(anvaya)*

tapasvī vālmīkiḥ tapaḥ-svādhyāya-nirataṁ vāg-vidāṁ varaṁ muni-puṅgavaṁ nāradaṁ paripapraccha |[4]

Translation

---

[3] According to the *Puranic Encyclopedia,* Vālmīki was the tenth son of the demigod Varuṇa but due to bad association became a dacoit and used to maintain himself and his family by robbing travellers. Once he happened to attack the seven great sages (saptarṣi), who then asked if his wife and children would share the reaction of his sinful deeds. Unable to answer, the thief went home and asked his family members if they were willing to share his sinful reactions, to which they declined. Undergoing a change of heart, he went before the sages and bowed down to them. Being pleased, the sages imparted spiritual knowledge to him and instructed him to perform austerities. He thus spent many years engaging in severe penances to the point that an anthill (valmīka) formed around his body. After a long time, the seven great sages returned and took him out of the anthill, and for this reason he became known as Vālmīki. He spent the rest of his life on the bank of the river Tamasā, where he met the sage Nārada. This whole account has been disputed by some scholars.

[4] In the prose order, all the external *saṁdhi* rules have been avoided, except those pertaining to the *anusvāra,* which are very easily apprehended.

The ascetic Vālmīki enquired from Nārada, the most exalted sage, who is always engaged in austerities and scriptural studies and is the best among those who know the Vedas.

तपस्वी महर्षि वाल्मीकि ने तपस्या और स्वाध्याय में लगे हुए, वेद वेत्ताओं में श्रेष्ठ, मुनिवर नारद से पूछा।

TEXT 2

को न्वस्मिन् साम्प्रतं लोके गुणवान् कश्च वीर्यवान् ।
धर्मज्ञश्च कृतज्ञश्च सत्यवाक्यो दृढव्रतः ॥ २ ॥

ko nv asmin sāmpratam̐ loke guṇavān kaś ca vīryavān |

dharma-jñaś ca kṛta-jñaś ca satya-vākyo dṛḍha-vrataḥ || 2 ||

kaḥ– (m. int. pron. nom. sg.) who; **nu**– (ind.) indeed; **asmin**– (d. pron. m. loc. sg.) in this; **sāmpratam**– (ind.) at present; **loke**– (m. n. loc. sg.) in the world; **guṇa**– (m. n.) virtue, good qualities; **vat**– (adj. aff.) possessing; **guṇavān**– (m. adj. nom. sg.) virtuous; **kaḥ**– (m. int. pron. nom. sg.) who; **ca**– (ind.) and; **vīrya**– (neu. n.) power, heroism; **vat**– (adj. aff.) possessing; **vīryavān**– (m. adj. nom. sg.) powerful; **dharma**– (m. n.) religious principles; **jña**– (adj.) knowing; **dharma-jñaḥ**– (tp. cp./m. adj. nom. sg.) knower of dharma; **ca**– (ind.) and; **kṛta**– (ppp./neu. n.) deed, service done; **jña**– (adj.) knowing, acknowledging; **kṛta-jñaḥ**– (tp. cp./m.

adj. nom. sg.) grateful; **ca**– (ind.) and; **satya**– (adj.) true; **vākya**– (neu. n.) speech; **satya-vākyaḥ**– (bv. cp./m. adj. nom. sg.) he whose speech is true; **dṛḍha**– (ppp./adj.) firm; **vrata**– (neu. n.) vow; **dṛḍha-vrataḥ**– (bv. cp./m. adj. nom. sg.) he whose vows are firm.

Prose order

sāmpratam asmin loke kaḥ nu guṇavān | kaḥ ca vīryavān dharma-jñaḥ ca kṛta-jñaḥ satya-vākyaḥ dṛḍha-vrataḥ ca |

Translation

Who in this world today is virtuous? Who is powerful and knows dharma? Who is grateful, truthful, and of firm vows?

इस समय इस लोक में कौन सचमुच गुणवान है? वीर्यवान्, धर्मज्ञ, कृतज्ञ, सत्यवादी और अपने व्रतों में दृढ़ कौन है?

TEXT 3

चारित्रेण च को युक्तः सर्वभूतेषु को हितः ।
विद्वान् कः कः समर्थश्च कश्चैकप्रियदर्शनः ॥ ३ ॥

cāritreṇa ca ko yuktaḥ sarva-bhūteṣu ko hitaḥ |

vidvān kaḥ kaḥ samarthaś ca kaś caika-priya-darśanaḥ || 3 ||

cāritreṇa– (neu. n. inst. sg.) by character; **ca**– (ind.) and; **kaḥ**– (m. int. pron. nom. sg.) who; **yuktaḥ**– (ppp./ m. adj. nom. sg.) endowed; **sarva**– (adj. pron.) all; **bhūta**– (neu. n.) living being; **sarva-bhūteṣu**– (tp. cp./neu. n. loc. pl.) towards all living beings; **kaḥ**– (m. int. pron. nom. sg.) who; **hitaḥ**– (m. adj. nom. sg.) kindly disposed; **vidvān**– (m. adj. nom. sg.) learned; **kaḥ**– (m. int. pron. nom. sg.) who; **kaḥ**– (m. int. pron. nom. sg.) who; **samarthaḥ**– (m. adj. nom. sg.) competent; **ca**– (ind.) and; **kaḥ**– (m. int. pron. nom. sg.) who; **ca**– (ind.) and; **eka**– (adj.) unique; **priya**– (adj.) pleasant; **darśana**– (neu. n.) appearance; **eka-priya-darśanaḥ**– (bv. cp./m. adj. nom. sg.) he whose appearance is uniquely pleasant.

Prose order

kaḥ ca cāritreṇa yuktaḥ | kaḥ sarva-bhūteṣu hitaḥ | kaḥ vidvān | kaḥ ca samarthaḥ | kaḥ ca eka-priya-darśanaḥ |

Translation

Who has good character traits? Who is kindly disposed towards all living beings? Who is learned and competent? Who has an appearance uniquely pleasant?

सदाचार युक्त कौन है? सब प्राणियों का हित करने वाला कौन है? विद्वान् कौन है? समर्थ कौन है? किसका दर्शन सब के लिये अद्वितीय सुखदायी है?

TEXT 4

आत्मवान् को जितक्रोधो द्युतिमान् कोऽनसूयकः ।

कस्य बिभ्यति देवाश्च जातरोषस्य संयुगे ॥ ४ ॥

ātmavān ko jita-krodho dyutimān[5] ko'nasūyakaḥ |

kasya bibhyati devāś ca jāta-roṣasya saṁyuge || 4 ||

ātman– (m. n.) self; **vat–** (adj. aff.) possessing; **ātmavān–** (m. adj. nom. sg.) self-possessed; **kaḥ–** (m. int. pron. nom. sg.) who; **jita–** (ppp./adj.) conquered; **krodha–** (m. n.) anger; **jita-krodhaḥ–** (bv. cp./m. adj. nom. sg.) he whose anger was conquered; **dyuti–** (f. n.) brightness; **mat–** (adj. aff.) possessing; **dyutimān–** (m. adj. nom. sg.) resplendent; **kaḥ–** (m. int. pron. nom. sg.) who; **anasūyakaḥ–** (m. adj. nom. sg.) devoid of envy; **kasya–** (m. int. pron. gen. sg.) whose; **bibhyati–** (√ bhī, pr. 3rd p. pl.) fear; **devāḥ–** (m. n. nom. pl.) the demigods; **ca–** (ind.) even; **jāta–** (ppp.) born, arisen; **roṣa–** (m. n.) wrath; **jāta-roṣasya–** (bv. cp./m. adj. gen. sg.) he whose wrath is arisen, enraged; **saṁyuge–** (m. n. loc. sg.) in battle.

Prose Order

kaḥ ātmavān jita-krodhaḥ | kaḥ dyutimān anasūyakaḥ | saṁyuge devāḥ ca kasya jāta-roṣasya bibhyati |

Translation

---

[5] Some editions read *matimān,* "thoughtful."

Who is self-possessed and has controlled his anger? Who is brilliant and non-envious? Who is feared even by the demigods when enraged in the battle?

आत्मवान और क्रोध को जीतने वाला कौन है? तेजस्वी और ईर्ष्या हीन कौन है? युद्ध में क्रुद्ध होने पर किससे देवता गण भी डरते हैं?

TEXT 5

एतदिच्छाम्यहं श्रोतुं परं कौतूहलं हि मे ।

महर्षे त्वं समर्थोऽसि ज्ञातुमेवंविधं नरम् ॥ ५ ॥

etad icchāmy ahaṁ śrotuṁ paraṁ kautūhalaṁ hi me |

maharṣe tvaṁ samartho'si jñātum evaṁ-vidhaṁ naram || 5 ||

etat– (neu. d. pron. acc. sg.) this; **icchāmi**– (√ iṣ, pr. 1st p. sg.) wish; **aham**– (1st p. pron. nom. sg.) I; **śrotum**– (inf. √ śru) to hear; **param**– (neu. adj. nom. sg.) greatest; **kautūhalam**– (neu. n. nom. sg.) curiosity; **hi**– (ind.) for; **me**– (1st p. pron. gen. sg.) my; **mahat**– (adj.) great; **ṛṣi**– (m. n.) sage; **maharṣe**– (tp. cp./m. n. voc. sg.) O great sage; **tvam**– (2nd p. pron. nom. sg.) you; **samarthaḥ**– (m. adj. nom. sg.) capable; **asi**– (√ as, pr. 2nd p. sg.) are; **jñātum**– (inf. √ jñā) to know; **evam**– (ind.) such; **vidhā**– (f. n.) kind; **evaṁ-vidham**– (tp. cp./m. adj. acc. sg.) of such a kind; **naram**– (m. n. acc. sg.) man.

Prose order

aham etat śrotum icchāmi hi me paraṁ kautūhalam | maharṣe tvam evaṁ-vidhaṁ naraṁ jñātuṁ samarthaḥ asi |

Translation

I wish to hear about this, for I have a great curiosity about this topic. O great sage, you are able to know such a person.

मैं यह सुनना चाहता हूँ, क्योंकि मुझे महान कौतूहल है। हे महर्षि, आप ऐसे पुरुष को जानने में समर्थ हैं।

TEXT 6

श्रुत्वा चैतत् त्रिलोकज्ञो वाल्मीकेर्नारदो वचः ।

श्रूयतामिति चामन्त्र्य प्रहृष्टो वाक्यमब्रवीत् ॥ ६ ॥

śrutvā caitat tri-loka-jño[6] vālmīker nārado vacaḥ |

śrūyatām iti cāmantrya prahṛṣṭo vākyam abravīt || 6 ||

śrutvā– (√ śru, abs.) having heard; **ca**– (ind.) and; **etat**– (neu. d. pron. acc. sg.) this; **tri**– (num.) three; **loka**– (m. n.) planetary system; **jña**– (adj.) knowing; **tri-loka-jñaḥ**– (tp. cp./m. adj. nom. sg.) knower of the three planetary systems; **vālmīkeḥ**– (m. n. gen. sg.) of Vālmīki; **nāradaḥ**– (m. n. nom. sg.) Nārada Muni; **vacaḥ**–

[6] Some editions read *tri-kāla-jñaḥ,* "knower of past, present and future."

(neu. n. acc. sg.) word; **śrūyatām**– (√ śru, ipt. 3rd p. sg.) hear; **iti**– (ind.) thus; **ca**– (ind.) and; **āmantrya**– (ā + √ mantr, abs.) having invited; **prahṛṣṭaḥ**– (ppp./ m. adj. nom. sg.) pleased; **vākyam**– (neu. n. acc. sg.) sentence, words; **abravīt**– (√ brū, imp. 3rd p. sg.) spoke.

Prose order

vālmīkeḥ etat vacaḥ ca śrutvā śrūyatām iti ca āmantrya prahṛṣṭaḥ tri-loka-jñaḥ nāradaḥ vākyam abravīt |

Translation

Having heard Vālmīki's words, Nārada Muni, knower of the three worlds, became pleased, and after inviting him to listen, spoke the following words.

वाल्मीकि का वचन सुनकर त्रिलोकों को जानने वाले नारद मुनि प्रसन्न हो गये। "सुनिये" — ऐसा कहकर वे अगले वाक्य बोले।

TEXT 7

बहवो दुर्लभाश्चैव ये त्वया कीर्तिता गुणाः ।
मुने वक्ष्याम्यहं बुद्धा तैर्युक्तः श्रूयतां नरः ॥७॥

bahavo durlabhāś caiva ye tvayā kīrtitā guṇāḥ |

mune vakṣyāmy ahaṁ buddhvā tair yuktaḥ śrūyatāṁ naraḥ ||7||

bahavaḥ– (m. adj. nom. pl.) many; **durlabhāḥ**– (m. adj. nom. pl.) difficult to be found; **ca**– (ind.) and; **eva**– (ind.) certainly; **ye**– (m. r. pron. nom. pl.) those who; **tvayā**– (2nd p. pron. inst. sg.) by you; **kīrtitāḥ**– (m. ppp. nom. pl.) mentioned; **guṇāḥ**– (m. n. nom. pl.) qualities; **mune**– (m. n. voc. sg.) O sage; **vakṣyāmi**– (√ vac, 1st p. fut. sg.) shall speak; **aham**– (1st p. pron. nom. sg.) I; **buddhvā**– (√ buddh, abs.) having known; **taiḥ**– (m. d. pron. inst. pl.) with those; **yuktaḥ**– (ppp./ m. adj. nom. sg.) endowed with; **śrūyatām**– (√ śru, ipt. 3rd p. sg.) hear; **naraḥ**– (m. n. nom. sg.) man.

Prose order

ye bahavaḥ guṇāḥ tvayā kīrtitāḥ durlabhāḥ ca eva | ahaṁ (taṁ) buddhvā vakṣyāmi | mune taiḥ yuktaḥ naraḥ śrūyatām |

Translation

These many qualities you mentioned are certainly very difficult to be found. O sage, hear about a person who has them, for having known Him myself, I shall now tell you.

जो सारे गुण आपने बताये हैं, वे अवश्य दुर्लभ हैं। हे मुनि, उस पुरुष के बारे में सुनिये, जो इन गुणों से युक्त है, क्योंकि मैं उसको जानता हूँ और आपको बताऊँगा।

TEXT 8

इक्ष्वाकुवंशप्रभवो रामो नाम जनैः श्रुतः ।

नियतात्मा महावीर्यो द्युतिमान् धृतिमान् वशी ॥ ८ ॥

ikṣvāku-vaṁśa-prabhavo rāmo nāma janaiḥ śrutaḥ |

niyatātmā mahā-vīryo dyutimān dhṛtimān vaśī || 8 ||

ikṣvāku– (m. n.) the sun-god named Ikṣvāku; **vaṁśa–** (m. n.) dynasty; **prabhava–** (m. n.) origin; **ikṣvāku-vaṁśa-prabhavaḥ–** (bv. cpd./ m. adj. nom. sg.) he whose origin is the dynasty of Ikṣvāku; **rāmaḥ–** (m. n. nom. sg.) Rāma; **nāma–** (ind.) by name; **janaiḥ–** (m. n. inst. pl.) by the people; **śrutaḥ–** (m. ppp. nom. sg.) known as; **niyata–** (ppp./adj.) restrained; **ātman–** (neu. n.) mind; **niyatātmā–** (bv. cpd./ m. adj. nom. sg.) he whose mind is restrained; **mahat–** (adj.) great; **vīrya–** (neu. n.) power; **mahā-vīryaḥ–** (bv. cpd./m. adj. nom. sg.) he whose power is great; **dyuti–** (f. n.) brightness; **mat–** (adj. aff.) possessing; **dyutimān–** (m. adj. nom. sg.) resplendent; **dhṛti–** (f. n.) steadiness; **mat–** (adj. aff.) possessing; **dhṛtimān–** (m. adj. nom. sg.) steadfast; **vaśī–** (m. adj. nom. sg.) self-controlled.

Prose order

ikṣvāku-vaṁśa-prabhavaḥ niyatātmā mahā-vīryaḥ dyutimān dhṛtimān vaśī rāmaḥ nāma janaiḥ śrutaḥ |

Translation

There is a very powerful person born in the dynasty of Ikṣvāku, [7] *known by the people as Rāma. With restrained mind, He is resplendent, steadfast and self-controlled.*

इक्ष्वाकु वंश में एक बहुत शक्तिशाली पुरुष उत्पन्न हुए हैं, जो अपना मन नियंत्रित रखने वाले, तेजस्वी, धैर्यवान और जितेन्द्रिय हैं। लोग उनको राम नाम से जानते हैं।

TEXT 9

बुद्धिमान् नीतिमान् वाग्मी श्रीमाञ् शत्रुनिबर्हणः ।

विपुलांसो महाबाहुः कम्बुग्रीवो महाहनुः ॥ ९ ॥

buddhimān nītimān vāgmī śrīmāñ śatru-nibarhaṇaḥ |

vipulāṁso mahā-bāhuḥ kambu-grīvo mahā-hanuḥ || 9 ||

buddhi– (f. n.) intelligence; **mat–** (adj. aff.) possessing; **buddhimān–** (m. adj. nom. sg.) intelligent; **nīti–** (f. n.) politics; **mat–** (adj. aff.) possessing; **nītimān–** (m. adj. nom. sg.) expert in politics; **vāgmī–** (m. adj. nom. sg.) eloquent; **śrī–** (f. n.) beauty; **mat–** (adj. aff.) possessing; **śrīmān–** (m. adj. nom. sg.) beautiful; **śatru–** (m. n.) enemy; **nibarhaṇa–** (neu. n.) destruction; **śatru-**

---

[7] Ikṣvāku was born from Vaivasvata Manu and is the head of the solar dynasty of kings on earth.

nibarhaṇaḥ– (tp. cpd./m. adj. nom. sg.) he who is the destruction of the enemies; **vipula**– (adj.) large; **aṁsa**– (m. n.) shoulder; **vipulāṁsaḥ**– (bv. cpd./m. adj. nom. sg.) he who has large shoulders; **mahat**– (adj.) long; **bāhu**– (m./f. n.) arm; **mahā-bāhuḥ**– (bv. cpd./m. adj. nom. sg.) he whose arms are long; **kambu**– (m. n.) conch; **grīva**– (m. n.) neck; **kambu-grīvaḥ**– (bv. cpd./m. adj. nom. sg.) he whose neck looks like a conch; **mahat**– (adj.) large; **hanu**– (neu. n.) cheek; **mahā-hanuḥ**– (bv. cpd./m. adj. nom. sg.) he who has large jaws.

Prose order

buddhimān nītimān vāgmī śrīmān śatru-nibarhaṇaḥ vipulāṁsaḥ mahā-bāhuḥ kambu-grīvaḥ mahā-hanuḥ |

Translation

He is intelligent, a wise politician, eloquent, beautiful and is the destroyer of the enemies. He has large shoulders, long arms, large cheeks, and His neck looks like a conch-shell.

वे बुद्धिमान, नीति निपुण, वाक्पटु, सुंदर, शत्रुओं का नाश करने वाले, विशाल कंधे वाले, लम्बी भुजाओं वाले, महती हनुवाले और शंख के समान कंठ वाले हैं।

TEXT 10

महोरस्को महेष्वासो गूढजत्रुररिंदमः ।

आजानुबाहुः सुशिराः सुललाटः सुविक्रमः ॥ १० ॥

mahorasko maheṣvāso gūḍha-jatrur ariṁ-damaḥ |

ā-jānu-bāhuḥ su-śirāḥ su-lalāṭaḥ su-vikramaḥ || 10 ||

mahat– (adj.) broad; **uras–** (neu. n.) chest; **mahoraskaḥ–** (bv. cpd./m. adj. nom. sg.) he whose chest is large; **mahat–** (adj.) big; **iṣvāsa–** (m. n.) bow; **maheṣvāsaḥ–** (bv. cpd./m. adj. nom. sg.) he whose bow is large; **gūḍha–** (ppp./adj.) concealed; **jatru–** (neu. n.) collar-bone; **gūḍha-jatruḥ–** (bv. cpd./m. adj. nom. sg.) he whose collar-bone is concealed (by muscles); **ari–** (m. n) enemy; **dama–** (adj.) subduing; **ariṁ-damaḥ–** (tp. cpd./m. adj. nom. sg.) the subduer of the enemies; **ā–** (aff.) up to; **jānu–** (neu. n.) knee; **bāhu–** (m./f. n.) arm; **ā-jānu-bāhuḥ–** (bv. cpd./m. adj. nom. sg.) he whose arms reach to the knees; **su–** (adj. aff.) beautiful; **śiras–** (neu. n.) head; **su-śirāḥ–** (bv. cpd./m. adj. nom. sg.) he whose head is beautiful; **su–** (adj. aff.) beautiful; **lalāṭa–** (neu. n.) forehead; **su-lalāṭaḥ–** (bv. cpd./m. adj. nom. sg.) he whose forehead is beautiful; **su–** (adj. aff.) beautiful; **vikrama–** (m. n.) gait; **su-vikramaḥ–** (bv. cpd./m. adj. nom. sg.) he whose gait is beautiful.

Prose order

mahoraskaḥ maheṣvāsaḥ gūḍha-jatruḥ ariṁ-damaḥ ā-jānu-bāhuḥ su-śirāḥ su-lalāṭaḥ su-vikramaḥ |

Translation

He has a broad chest and holds a large bow. His collar-bone is covered by muscles and He is the subduer of enemies. His arms reach to His knees, and His head, forehead and gait are very lovely.

वे विशाल वक्ष वाले, महान धनुष वाले हैं और उनकी हँसली की हड्डी छिपी हुई है। वे शत्रुओं का दमन करने वाले हैं। उनकी भुजाएँ घुटनों तक लम्बी हैं और उनके मस्तक, ललाट और गति सुंदर हैं।

TEXT 11

समः समविभक्ताङ्गः स्निग्धवर्णः प्रतापवान् ।

पीनवक्षा विशालाक्षो लक्ष्मीवाञ् छुभलक्षणः ॥ ११ ॥

samaḥ sama-vibhaktāṅgaḥ snigdha-varṇaḥ pratāpavān |

pīna-vakṣā viśālākṣo lakṣmīvāñ chubha-lakṣaṇaḥ || 11 ||

samaḥ– (m. adj. nom. sg.) equipoised; **sama**– (adj.) proportionate; **vibhakta**– (ppp./adj.) divided; **aṅga**– (neu. n.) limb; **sama-vibhaktāṅgaḥ**– (bv. cpd./m. adj. nom. sg.) he whose limbs are proportionately divided; **snigdha**– (ppp./adj.) shining; **varṇa**– (m. n.) colour; **snigdha-varṇaḥ**– (bv. cpd./m. adj. nom. sg.) he whose colour is resplendent; **pratāpa**– (m. n.) strength; **vat**– (adj. aff.) possessing; **pratāpavān**– (m. adj. nom. sg.)

possessing strength; **pīna**– (ppp./adj.) muscular; **vakṣas**– (neu. n.) chest; **pīna-vakṣāḥ**– (bv. cpd./m. adj. nom. sg.) he whose chest is muscular; **viśāla**– (adj.) large; **akṣa**– (neu. n.) eye; **viśālākṣaḥ**– (bv. cpd./m. adj. nom. sg.) he whose eyes are large; **lakṣmī**– (f. n.) fortune; **vat**– (adj. aff.) possessing; **lakṣmīvān**– (m. adj. nom. sg.) prosperous; **śubha**– (adj.) auspicious; **lakṣaṇa**– (neu. n.) characteristic; **śubha-lakṣaṇaḥ**– (bv. cpd./m. adj. nom. sg.) he whose characteristics are auspicious.

Prose order

samaḥ sama-vibhaktāṅgaḥ snigdha-varṇaḥ pratāpavān pīna-vakṣāḥ viśālākṣaḥ lakṣmīvān śubha-lakṣaṇaḥ |

Translation

He is equipoised, His limbs are proportionate and His bodily hue is shining. He is very strong and has a muscular chest and large eyes. He is prosperous and has auspicious characteristics.

वे समचित्त हैं, उनके शरीर के अंग समान रूप से विभक्त हैं और उनका रंग चमकदार है। वे प्रतापी हैं और उनका वक्षस्थल मांसल है। वे विशाल नेत्र वाले, लक्ष्मी और शुभ लक्षणों से संपन्न हैं।

TEXT 12

धर्मज्ञः सत्यसंधश्च प्रजानां च हिते रतः ।

यशस्वी ज्ञानसम्पन्नः शुचिर्वश्यः समाधिमान् ॥ १२ ॥

dharma-jñaḥ satya-saṁdhaś ca prajānāṁ ca hite rataḥ |

yaśasvī jñāna-sampannaḥ śucir vaśyaḥ samādhimān || 12 ||

dharma- (m.n.) religion, duty; **jña-** (adj.) knower; **dharma-jñaḥ-** (tp. cp./m. adj. nom. sg.) knower of duty; **satya-** (adj.) true; **saṁdhā-** (f. n.) promise; **satya-saṁdhaḥ**[8]- (bv. cp./m. adj. nom. sg.) he whose promises are true; **ca-** (ind.) and; **prajānām-** (f. n. gen. pl.) of the people; **ca-** (ind.) and; **hite-** (neu. n. loc. sg.) in the welfare; **rataḥ-** (ppp./m. adj. nom. sg.) attached; **yaśasvī-** (m. adj. nom. sg.) famous; **jñāna-** (neu. n.) knowledge; **sampanna-** (ppp./adj.) endowed with; **jñāna-sampannaḥ-** (tp. cp./m. adj. nom. sg.) endowed with knowledge; **śuciḥ-** (m. adj. nom. sg.) pure; **vaśyaḥ-** (m. adj. nom. sg.) subdued; **samādhi-** (m. n.) concentration of the mind; **mat-** (adj. aff.) possessing; **samādhimān-** (tp. cp./m. adj. nom. sg.) having a concentrated mind.

Prose order

dharma-jñaḥ satya-saṁdhaḥ prajānāṁ ca hite rataḥ yaśasvī jñāna-sampannaḥ śuciḥ vaśyaḥ samādhimān ca |

---

[8] The word *saṁdhā* is feminine, but here it becomes masculine because the last word of a *bahuvrīhi* compound follows the gender of the subject it qualifies.

Translation

He knows dharma and is true to His promises, attached to the interest of the people, famous, knowledgeable, pure, self-controlled and of concentrated mind.

वे धर्म के ज्ञाता, सत्यप्रतिज्ञ, प्रजा के हित में संलग्न, यशस्वी, ज्ञानसंपन्न, शुद्ध, आत्मवश्य और समाधि में निष्ठ हैं।

TEXT 13

प्रजापतिसमः श्रीमान् धाता रिपुनिषूदनः ।

रक्षिता जीवलोकस्य धर्मस्य परिरक्षिता ॥ १३ ॥

prajāpati-samaḥ śrīmān dhātā ripu-niṣūdanaḥ |

rakṣitā jīva-lokasya dharmasya parirakṣitā || 13 ||

prajāpati– (m. n.) the progenitor, Lord Brahmā; **sama–** (adj.) like; **prajāpati-samaḥ–** (tp. cp./m. adj. nom. sg.) like Lord Brahmā; **śrī–** (f. n.) fortune; **mat–** (adj. aff.) possessing; **śrīmān–** (m. adj. nom. sg.) possessing all fortune; **dhātā–** (m. n. nom. sg.) maintainer; **ripu–** (m. n.) enemy; **niṣūdana–** (m. n.) annihilator; **ripu-niṣūdanaḥ–** (tp. cp./m. adj. nom. sg.) the annihilator of the enemies; **rakṣitā–** (m. adj. nom. sg.) the protector; **jīva–** (m. n.) the living entity; **loka–** (m. n.) the world; **jīva-lokasya–** (tp. cp./m. n. gen. sg.) of the world of the living entities; **dharmasya–**

(m. n. gen. sg.) of dharma; **parirakṣitā–** (m. adj. nom. sg.) the protector.

Prose order

prajāpati-samaḥ śrīmān dhātā ripu-niṣūdanaḥ jīva-lokasya rakṣitā dharmasya parirakṣitā |

Translation

He is like Lord Brahmā and possesses all good fortune. He is the annihilator of the enemies, the maintainer, the protector of the world of the living entities and the guardian of dharma.

वे ब्रह्मा के तुल्य, श्री संपन्न, पालन करने वाले, शत्रु का नाश करने वाले, जीवों और धर्म के रक्षक हैं।

TEXT 14

रक्षिता स्वस्य धर्मस्य स्वजनस्य च रक्षिता ।

वेदवेदाङ्गतत्त्वज्ञो धनुर्वेदे च निष्ठितः ॥ १४ ॥

rakṣitā svasya dharmasya sva-janasya ca rakṣitā |

veda-vedāṅga-tattva-jño dhanur-vede ca niṣṭhitaḥ || 14 ||

rakṣitā– (m. adj. nom. sg.) protector; **svasya–** (m. adj. gen. sg.) His own; **dharmasya–** (m. n. gen. sg.) duty; **sva-janasya–** (tp.

cp./m. n. gen. sg.) of His own people; **ca**– (ind.) and; **rakṣitā**– (m. adj. nom. sg.) protector; **veda**– (m. n.) the Vedas; **vedāṅga**– (neu. n.) the six auxiliary Vedic texts[9]; **tattva**– (neu. n.) the truth; **jña**– (adj.) knower; **veda-vedāṅga-tattva-jñaḥ**– (tp. cp./m. adj. nom. sg.) knower of the truth of the Vedas and Vedāṅgas; **dhanuḥ**– (neu. n.) bow; **veda**– (m. n.) the Veda; **dhanur-vede**– (tp. cp./m. n. loc. sg.) in the Dhanur-veda, the military science; **ca**– (ind.) and; **niṣṭhitaḥ**– (ppp./m. adj. nom. sg.) skilled in.

Prose order

svasya dharmasya rakṣitā sva-janasya ca rakṣitā veda-vedāṅga-tattva-jñaḥ dhanur-vede niṣṭhitaḥ ca |

Translation

Śrī Rāma is the protector of His own dharma and of His people. He knows the truth of the Vedas and Vedāṅgas, and is skilled in the Dhanur-veda.

श्री राम अपने धर्म के रक्षक और अपने जन के रक्षक भी हैं। वे वेदों और वेदांगों के तत्त्व के ज्ञाता हैं और धनुर्वेद में निपुण हैं।

---

9 *Vyākaraṇa* (grammar), *nirukta* (etymology), *śikṣā* (phonetics), *chandaḥ* (prosody), *jyotiṣa* (astronomy) and *kalpa* (sacrificial rules).

TEXT 15

सर्वशास्त्रार्थतत्त्वज्ञः स्मृतिमान् प्रतिभानवान् ।

सर्वलोकप्रियः साधुरदीनात्मा विचक्षणः ॥ १५ ॥

sarva-śāstrārtha-tattva-jñaḥ smṛtimān pratibhānavān |

sarva-loka-priyaḥ sādhur adīnātmā vicakṣaṇaḥ || 15 ||

sarva– (adj. pron.) all; **śāstra–** (neu. n.) scripture; **artha–** (m. n.) meaning; **tattva–** (neu. n.) the truth; **jña–** (m. adj.) knower; **sarva-śāstrārtha-tattva-jñaḥ–** (tp. cp./ m. adj. nom. sg.) knower of the truth and meaning of all scriptures; **smṛti–** (f. n.) memory; **mat–** (adj. aff.) possessing; **smṛtimān–** (m. adj. nom. sg.) having good memory; **pratibhāna–** (neu. n.) brilliant intelligence; **vat–** (adj. aff.) having; **pratibhānavān–** (m. adj. nom. sg.) having brilliant intelligence; **sarva–** (adj. pron.) all; **loka–** (m. n.) people; **priya–** (adj.) dear; **sarva-loka-priyaḥ–** (tp. cp./m. adj. nom. sg.) dear to all the people; **sādhuḥ–** (m. adj. nom. sg.) righteous; **adīna–** (adj.) not dejected; **ātman–** (neu. n.) mind; **adīnātmā–** (bv. cp./m. adj. nom. sg.) he whose mind is never dejected; **vicakṣaṇaḥ–** (m. adj. nom. sg.) learned.

Prose order

sarva-śāstrārtha-tattva-jñaḥ smṛtimān pratibhānavān sarva-loka-priyaḥ sādhuḥ adīnātmā vicakṣaṇaḥ |

Translation

He knows the truth and meaning of all scriptures and has good memory. He is dear to all the people, righteous, highly intelligent, learned and never of dejected mind.

वे सब शास्त्रों के अर्थ और तत्त्व के ज्ञाता, स्मरण शक्ति से युक्त, तीक्ष्ण बुद्धि, सब लोगों के प्रिय, साधु तथा पंडित हैं और उनका मन कभी उदास नहीं होता।

TEXT 16

सर्वदाभिगतः सद्भिः समुद्र इव सिन्धुभिः ।

आर्यः सर्वसमश्चैव सदैव प्रियदर्शनः ॥ १६ ॥

sarvadābhigataḥ sadbhiḥ samudra iva sindhubhiḥ |

āryaḥ sarva-samaś caiva sadaiva priya-darśanaḥ || 16 ||

sarvadā– (ind.) always; **abhigataḥ**– (ppp. m. nom. sg.) approached; **sadbhiḥ**– (m. n. inst. pl.) by the saints; **samudraḥ**– (m. n. nom. sg.) ocean; **iva**– (ind.) like; **sindhubhiḥ**– (f. n. inst. pl.) rivers; **āryaḥ**– (m. adj. nom. sg.) respectable; **sarva**– (adj. pron.) all; **sama**– (adj.) equal; **sarva-samaḥ**– (tp. cp./m. adj. nom. sg.) equal to all; **ca**– (ind.) and; **eva**– (ind.) indeed; **sadā**– (ind.) always; **eva**– (ind.) certainly; **priya**– (adj.) pleasant; **darśana**– (neu. n.) appearance; **priya-darśanaḥ**– (bv. cp./m. adj. nom. sg.) he whose appearance is pleasant.

Prose order

samudraḥ iva sindhubhiḥ sarvadā sadbhiḥ abhigataḥ āryaḥ sarva-samaḥ ca eva sadā eva priya-darśanaḥ |

Translation

Just as the ocean is approached by rivers, He is approached by saintly people at all times. He is equal to all and His appearance is always pleasant.

साधु गण हमेशा उनके पास जाते हैं जैसे नदियाँ समुद्र के पास जाती हैं। वे सब के प्रति सम हैं और सदैव प्रियदर्शन हैं।

TEXT 17

स च सर्वगुणोपेतः कौसल्यानन्दवर्धनः ।
समुद्र इव गाम्भीर्ये धैर्येण हिमवानिव ॥ १७ ॥
sa ca sarva-guṇopetaḥ kausalyānanda-vardhanaḥ |

samudra iva gāmbhīrye dhairyeṇa himavān iva || 17 ||

saḥ– (3rd p. pron. nom. m. sg.) He; **ca**– (ind.) and; **sarva**– (adj. pron.) all; **guṇa**– (m. n.) virtue; **upeta**– (ppp./adj.) endowed with; **sarva-guṇopetaḥ**– (tp. cp./m. adj. nom. sg.) endowed with all virtues; **kausalyā**– (f. n.) Queen Kausalyā[10]; **ānanda**– (m. n.) joy;

---

[10] Also spelled 'Kauśalyā.' She is the senior queen of the kingdom of Ayodhyā and Rāma's mother.

vardhana– (adj.) increasing; **kausalyānanda-vardhanaḥ**– (tp. cp./m. adj. nom. sg.) He Who increases Kausalyā's joy; **samudraḥ**– (m. n. nom. sg.) the ocean; **iva**– (ind.) like; **gāmbhīrye**– (neu. n. loc. sg.) in depth; **dhairyeṇa**– (neu. n. inst. sg.) in steadfastness; **hima**– (neu. n.) snow; **vat**– (adj. aff.) having; **himavān**– (m. n. nom. sg.) the Himālayas; **iva**– (ind.) like.

Prose order

saḥ sarva-guṇopetaḥ kausalyānanda-vardhanaḥ ca | gāmbhīrye samudraḥ iva dhairyeṇa himavān iva |

Translation

He has all virtues and He increases Queen Kauśalyā's joy. His depth is like the ocean and His steadfastness is like the Himālayas.

वे सब गुणों से संपन्न हैं और महारानी कौशल्या का आनंद वर्धन करते हैं। गाम्भीर्य में वे समुद्र के समान हैं और धैर्य में हिमालय के समान।

TEXT 18

विष्णुना सद्दशो वीर्ये सोमवत् प्रियदर्शनः ।

कालाग्निसद्दशः क्रोधे क्षमया पृथिवीसमः ॥ १८ ॥

धनदेन समस्त्यागे सत्ये धर्म इवापरः ।

viṣṇunā sadṛśo vīrye somavat priya-darśanaḥ |

kālāgni-sadṛśaḥ krodhe kṣamayā pṛthivī-samaḥ || 18 ||

dhanadena samas tyāge satye dharma ivāparaḥ |

viṣṇunā– (m. n. inst. sg.) with Lord Viṣṇu; **sadṛśaḥ**– (m. adj. nom. sg.) similar; **vīrye**– (neu. n. loc. sg.) in strength; **soma**– (m. n.) the moon-god; **vat**– (adj. aff.) like; **somavat**– (ind. adj.) like the moon; **priya**– (adj.) pleasant; **darśana**– (neu. n.) appearance; **priya-darśanaḥ**– (bv. cp./m. adj. nom. sg.) he whose appearance is pleasant; **kāla**– (m. n.) time, death; **agni**– (m. n.) fire; **sadṛśa**– (adj.) similar; **kālāgni-sadṛśaḥ**– (tp. cp./m. adj. nom. sg.) like the fire of devastation; **krodhe**– (m. n. loc. sg.) in rage; **kṣamayā**– (f. n. inst. sg.) in forbearance; **pṛthivī**– (f. n.) the earth; **sama**– (adj.) equal; **pṛthivī-samaḥ**– (tp. cp./m. adj. nom. sg.) like the earth; **dhanadena**– (m. n. inst. sg.) with Kuvera; **samaḥ**– (m. adj. nom. sg.) equal; **tyāge**– (m. n. loc. sg.) in giving in charity; **satye**– (neu. n. loc. sg.) in truthfulness; **dharmaḥ**– (m. n. nom. sg.) Yamarāja; **iva**– (ind.) like; **aparaḥ**– (m. adj. nom. sg.) another.

Prose order

vīrye viṣṇunā sadṛśaḥ somavat priya-darśanaḥ krodhe kālāgni-sadṛśaḥ kṣamayā pṛthivī-samaḥ tyāge dhanadena samaḥ satye aparaḥ dharmaḥ iva |

Translation

He is similar to Lord Viṣṇu[11] *in strength and His appearance is pleasant like the moon. In rage, He is like the fire of devastation, in forbearance, He is like the earth, in giving in charity, He is like Kuvera,*[12] *and in truthfulness, He is like another Yamarāja.*[13]

वीर्य में वे भगवान विष्णु के समान हैं और सोम जैसे प्रियदर्शन। क्रोध में वे कालाग्नि जैसे हैं, क्षमा में वे पृथ्वी जैसे, दान में कुवेर जैसे और सत्य में मानो दूसरे यमराज।

---

[11] According to the *Vālmīki Rāmāyaṇa* (1.17.6), Rāma is an avatar of Lord Viṣṇu: *kausalyā janayad rāmaṁ divya-lakṣaṇa-saṁyutam, viṣṇor ardhaṁ mahā-bhāgaṁ putram ikṣvāku-nandanam,* "Then Queen Kausalyā gave birth to Rāma, a plenary portion of Lord Viṣṇu, Who thus appeared as her son with all divine characteristics to give joy to the dynasty of Ikṣvāku." In his commentary named *Rāmāyaṇa-tilaka*, Nāgojī Bhaṭṭa explains that here we have an *ananvayālaṅkāra*, a figure of expression in which the object and subject of a comparison are the same. Lord Viṣṇu is described as *asamordhva*, one Who has no equal or superior, so it is appropriate that He be compared to Himself.

[12] King of the Yakṣas and treasurer in the heavenly planets.

[13] Yamarāja or Dharmarāja is the superintendent of death and justice.

Ayodhyā-kāṇḍa

TEXTS 19 - 20

तमेवंगुणसम्पन्नं रामं सत्यपराक्रमम् ॥ १९ ॥

ज्येष्ठं श्रेष्ठगुणैर्युक्तं प्रियं दशरथः सुतम् ।

प्रकृतीनां हितैर्युक्तं प्रकृतिप्रियकाम्यया ॥ २० ॥

यौवराज्येन संयोक्तुमैच्छत् प्रीत्या महीपतिः ।

tam evaṁ-guṇa-sampannaṁ rāmaṁ satya-parākramam || 19 ||

jyeṣṭhaṁ śreṣṭha-guṇair yuktaṁ priyaṁ daśarathaḥ sutam |

prakṛtīnāṁ hitair yuktaṁ prakṛti-priya-kāmyayā || 20 ||

yauvarājyena saṁyoktum aicchat prītyā mahī-patiḥ |

tam– (3rd p. pron. acc. m. sg.) to him; **evam**– (ind.) such; **guṇa**– (m. n.) qualities; **sampanna**– (ppp./ adj.) endowed with; **evaṁ-guṇa-sampannam**– (tp. cp./m. adj. acc. sg.) endowed with such qualities; **rāmam**– (m. n. acc. sg.) to Śrī Rāma; **satya**– (adj.) real; **parākrama**– (m. n.) prowess; **satya-parākramam**– (bv. cp./m. adj. acc. sg.) to him whose prowess is real; **jyeṣṭham**– (m. adj. acc. sg.) eldest; **śreṣṭha**– (adj.) best; **guṇa**– (m. n.) virtues; **śreṣṭha-guṇaiḥ**– (tp. cp./m. adj. inst. pl.) with the most exalted virtues; **yuktam**– (ppp./m. adj. acc. sg.) endowed with; **priyam**–

(m. adj. acc. sg.) dear; **daśarathaḥ**– (m. n. nom. sg.) King Daśaratha; **sutam**– (m. n. acc. sg.) son; **prakṛtīnām**– (f. n. gen. pl.) of the people; **hitaiḥ**– (neu. n. inst. pl.) with a kind disposition; **yuktam**– (ppp./m. adj. acc. sg.) endowed with; **prakṛti**– (f. n.) subjects; **priya**– (neu. n) favour; **kāmyā**– (f. n.) desire; **prakṛti-priya-kāmyayā**– (tp. cp. f. inst. sg) with the desire to please the subjects; **yauvarājyena**– (neu. n. inst. sg.) as the heir-apparent; **saṁyoktum**– (inf. sam + √yuñj) to appoint; **aicchat**– (√iṣ, imp. 3rd p. sg.) wished; **prītyā**– (f. n. inst. sg.) out of affection; **mahī**– (f. n.) the earth; **pati**– (m. n.) lord; **mahī-patiḥ**– (tp. cp./m. n. nom. sg.) king.

Prose order

prakṛti-priya-kāmyayā mahī-patiḥ daśarathaḥ tam evaṁ-guṇa-sampannaṁ satya-parākramaṁ jyeṣṭhaṁ śreṣṭha-guṇaiḥ yuktaṁ prakṛtīnāṁ hitaiḥ yuktaṁ priyaṁ sutaṁ rāmaṁ prītyā yauvarājyena saṁyoktum aicchat |

Translation

Out of affection and a desire to please his subjects, King Daśaratha desired to appoint his dear son Rāma as the heir-apparent. Rāma, his eldest son, has all the mentioned qualities and true heroism. He has exalted virtues and is very kindly disposed towards the subjects.

स्नेह से और प्रजा को प्रसन्न करने की इच्छा से महाराज दशरथ ने अपने प्रिय पुत्र राम को युवराज नियुक्त करना चाहा, जो सचमुच पराक्रमी, इन सब गुणों से संपन्न, ज्येष्ठ, उत्तम गुणों से युक्त और प्रजा का हित करने वाले हैं।

TEXTS 21 - 22

तस्याभिषेकसम्भारान् दृष्ट्वा भार्याथ कैकयी ॥ २१ ॥

पूर्वं दत्तवरा देवी वरमेनमयाचत ।

विवासनं च रामस्य भरतस्याभिषेचनम् ॥ २२ ॥

tasyābhiṣeka-sambhārān dṛṣṭvā bhāryātha kaikayī || 21 ||

pūrvaṁ datta-varā devī varam enam ayācata |

vivāsanaṁ ca rāmasya bharatasyābhiṣecanam || 22 ||

tasya– (3rd p. pron. gen. m. sg.) His; **abhiṣeka**– (m. n.) consecration; **sambhāra**– (m. n.) preparation; **abhiṣeka-sambhārān**– (tp. cp. m. acc. pl.) the preparations for the consecration; **dṛṣṭvā**– (abs. √ dṛś) having seen; **bhāryā**– (f. n. nom. sg.) the wife; **atha**– (ind.) then; **kaikayī**– (f. n. nom. sg.) Queen Kaikayī[14]; **pūrvam**– (ind.) previously; **datta**– (ppp.) given;

[14] The youngest queen of Ayodhyā, also spelled 'Kaikeyī.' Once during a battle, she saved the King's life, who then granted her two wishes. She

vara– (m. n.) benediction; **datta-varā**– (bv. cp./f. adj. nom. sg.) she who was given a benediction; **devī**– (f. n. nom. sg.) lady; **varam**– (m. n. acc. sg.) a benediction; **enam**– (m. d. pron. acc. sg.) this; **ayācata**– (√ yāc, imp. 3rd p. sg.) asked; **vivāsanam**– (neu. n. acc. sg.) exile; **ca**– (ind.) and; **rāmasya**– (m. n. gen. sg.) of Śrī Rāma; **bharatasya**– (m. n. gen. sg.) of Bharata; **abhiṣecanam**– (neu. n. acc. sg.) the consecration.

Prose order

atha tasya abhiṣeka-sambhārān dṛṣṭvā pūrvaṁ datta-varā bhāryā devī kaikayī rāmasya vivāsanaṁ bharatasya ca abhiṣecanam enaṁ varam ayācata |

Translation

Having seen the preparations for Rāma's consecration, Queen Kaikeyī, the youngest wife of King Daśaratha, who had been given a benediction by him on a previous occasion, took the opportunity to ask for the exile of Rāma and the consecration of her son, Bharata.

महाराज दशरथ की कनिष्ठ पत्नी कैकेयी देवी ने, जिनको पहले उन्होंने दो वर देने की प्रतिज्ञा की थी, राम के अभिषेक की तैयारी देखकर राम का वनवास और अपने पुत्र भरत का राज्याभिषेक मांगे।

---

preferred to ask him to fulfil these wishes later on when she finds a suitable moment.

TEXT 23

स सत्यवचनाद्राजा धर्मपाशेन संयतः ।

विवासयामास सुतं रामं दशरथः प्रियम् ॥ २३ ॥

sa satya-vacanād rājā dharma-pāśena saṁyataḥ |

vivāsayām āsa sutaṁ rāmaṁ daśarathaḥ priyam || 23 ||

saḥ– (3rd p. pron. nom. m. sg.) he; **satya**– (adj.) true; **vacana**– (neu. n.) speech; **satya-vacanāt**– (tp. cp. neu. abl. sg.) due to speaking the truth; **rājā**– (m. n. nom. sg.) the King; **dharma**– (m. n.) the religious principles; **pāśa**– (m. n.) tie; **dharma-pāśena**– (tp. cp. m. inst. sg.) by the tie of dharma; **saṁyataḥ**– (ppp./m. adj. nom. sg.) bound; **vivāsayām āsa**– (vi + vāsay[15], perf. 3rd p. sg.) sent into exile; **sutam**– (m. n. acc. sg.) son; **rāmam**– (m. n. acc. sg.) Śrī Rāma; **daśarathaḥ**– (m. n. nom. sg.) King Daśaratha; **priyam**– (m. adj. acc. sg.) dear.

Prose order

satya-vacanāt dharma-pāśena saṁyataḥ saḥ rājā daśarathaḥ priyaṁ sutaṁ rāmaṁ vivāsayām āsa |

---

[15] This is the causative verbal form of the root *vas*.

Translation

Being true to his word and bound by dharma, King Daśaratha sent his dear son Rāma into exile.

सत्यवादी होने के कारण, धर्मपाश से बद्ध महाराज दशरथ ने अपने प्रिय पुत्र राम को वनवास के लिए भेजा।

TEXT 24

स जगाम वनं वीरः प्रतिज्ञामनुपालयन् ।

पितुर्वचननिर्देशात् कैकेय्याः प्रियकारणात् ॥ २४ ॥

sa jagāma vanaṁ vīraḥ pratijñām anupālayan |

pitur vacana-nirdeśāt kaikeyyāḥ priya-kāraṇāt || 24 ||

saḥ– (3rd p. pron. nom. m. sg.) He; **jagāma**– (√gam, per. 3rd p. sg.) went; **vanam**– (neu. n. acc. sg.) to the forest; **vīraḥ**– (m. n. nom. sg.) the hero; **pratijñām**– (f. n. acc. sg.) the promise; **anupālayan**– (anu + √pāl, m. prp. nom. sg.) maintaining; **pituḥ**– (m. n. gen. sg.) of His father; **vacana**– (neu. n.) speech; **nirdeśa**– (m. n.) command; **vacana-nirdeśāt**– (tp. cp. m. abl. sg.) by the command of his word; **kaikeyyāḥ**– (f. n. gen. sg.) of Kayikeyī; **priya**– (neu. n.) favour; **kāraṇa**– (neu. n.) cause; **priya-kāraṇāt**– (tp. cp. neu. abl. sg.) in order to favour.

Prose order

kaikeyyāḥ priya-kāraṇāt pituḥ vacana-nirdeśāt pratijñām anupālayan saḥ vīraḥ vanaṁ jagāma |

Translation

Because of the verbal command of His father and to please Kaikeyī, the hero Rāma went to the forest maintaining the promise.

अपने पिता की आज्ञा से और कैकेयी को प्रसन्न करने की प्रतिज्ञा का पालन करते हुए वीर राम वन चले गए।

TEXT 25

तं व्रजन्तं प्रियो भ्राता लक्ष्मणोऽनुजगाम ह ।

स्नेहाद् विनयसम्पन्नः सुमित्रानन्दवर्धनः ॥ २५ ॥

भ्रातरं दयितो भ्रातुः सौभ्रात्रमनुदर्शयन् ।

taṁ vrajantaṁ priyo bhrātā lakṣmaṇo'nujagāma ha |

snehād vinaya-sampannaḥ sumitrānanda-vardhanaḥ || 25 ||

bhrātaraṁ dayito bhrātuḥ saubhrātram anudarśayan |

tam– (3rd p. pron. acc. m. sg.) to Him; **vrajantam**– (√ vraj, m. prp. acc. sg.) going; **priyaḥ**– (m. adj. nom. sg.) affectionate; **bhrātā**– (m. n. nom. sg.) brother; **lakṣmaṇaḥ**– (m. n. nom. sg.) Prince Lakṣmaṇa; **anujagāma**– (anu +√ gam, per. 3rd p. sg.) followed; **ha**– (ind.) indeed; **snehāt**– (m. n. abl. sg.) out of love; **vinaya**– (m. n.) humbleness; **sampanna**– (ppp./adj.) endowed with; **vinaya-sampannaḥ**– (tp. cp./m. adj. nom. sg.) endowed with humbleness; **sumitrā**– (f. n.) Queen Sumitrā[16]; **ānanda**– (m. n.) joy; **vardhana**– (adj.) increasing; **sumitrānanda-vardhanaḥ**– (tp. cp./m. adj. nom. sg.) he who increases the joy of Sumitrā; **bhrātaram**– (m. n. acc. sg.) to his brother; **dayitaḥ**– (m. adj. nom. sg.) beloved; **bhrātuḥ**– (m. n. gen. sg.) of his brother; **saubhrātram**– (neu. n. acc. sg.) brotherhood; **anudarśayan**– (anu + darśay[17], m. prp. nom. sg.) showing.

Prose order

bhrātuḥ priyaḥ dayitaḥ bhrātā vinaya-saṁpannaḥ sumitrānanda-vardhanaḥ lakṣmaṇaḥ bhrātaraṁ saubhrātram anudarśayan snehāt vrajantaṁ tam anujagāma ha |

Translation

---

[16] One of the three wives of King Daśaratha.

[17] This is the causative verbal form of the root *dṛś*.

When Śrī Rāma was going away, His beloved and affectionate brother Lakṣmaṇa, who is very humble and who increases the joy of his mother Sumitrā, followed Him out of love, thus showing his brotherly affection.

जब श्री राम जा रहे थे, उनके प्यारे और प्रिय भाई लक्ष्मण ने, जो बहुत विनीत हैं और अपनी माता सुमित्रा के आनंद वर्धक हैं, अपने भ्रातृ भाव का प्रदर्शन करते हुए, स्नेह से उनका अनुसरण किया।

TEXTS 26 - 28

रामस्य दयिता भार्या नित्यं प्राणसमा हिता ॥ २६ ॥
जनकस्य कुले जाता देवमायेव निर्मिता ।
सर्वलक्षणसम्पन्ना नारीणामुत्तमा वधूः ॥ २७ ॥
सीताप्यनुगता रामं शशिनं रोहिणी यथा ।
पौरैरनुगतो दूरं पित्रा दशरथेन च ॥ २८ ॥

rāmasya dayitā bhāryā nityaṁ prāṇa-samā hitā || 26 ||

janakasya kule jātā deva-māyeva nirmitā |

sarva-lakṣaṇa-sampannā nārīṇām uttamā vadhūḥ || 27 ||

sītāpy anugatā rāmaṁ śaśinaṁ rohiṇī yathā |

paurair anugato dūraṁ pitrā daśarathena ca || 28 ||

rāmasya– (m. n. gen. sg.) of Rāma; **dayitā**– (f. adj. nom. sg.) beloved; **bhāryā**– (f. n. nom. sg.) wife; **nityam**– (ind.) always; **prāṇa**– (m. n.) life; **sama**– (adj.) equal; **prāṇa-samā**– (tp. cp./f. adj. nom. sg.) she who is equal to His life; **hitā**– (f. adj. nom. sg.) affectionate; **janakasya**– (m. n. gen. sg.) of King Janaka[18]; **kule**– (neu. n. loc. sg.) in the house; **jātā**– (ppp. f. nom. sg.) born; **deva**– (m. n.) God; **māyā**– (f. n.) the internal potency; **deva-māyā**– (tp. cp./f. n. nom. sg.) the internal potency of God; **iva**– (ind.) like; **nirmitā**– (f. adj. nom. sg.) made; **sarva**– (adj. pron.) all; **lakṣaṇa**– (neu. n.) characteristic; **sampanna**– (ppp./adj.) endowed with; **sarva-lakṣaṇa-sampannā**– (tp. cp./f. adj. nom. sg.) endowed with all good characteristics; **nārīṇām**– (f. n. gen. pl.) of women; **uttamā**– (f. adj. nom. sg.) best; **vadhūḥ**– (f. n. nom. sg.) wife; **sītā**– (f. n. nom. sg.) called Sītā; **api**– (ind.) also; **anugatā**– (ppp. f. nom. sg.) followed; **rāmam**– (m. n. acc. sg.) to Śrī Rāma; **śaśinam**– (m. n. acc. sg.) the moon; **rohiṇī**– (f. n. nom. sg.) the constellation Rohiṇī[19]; **yathā**– (ind.) just as; **pauraiḥ**– (m. n. inst. pl.) by the citizens; **anugataḥ**– (ppp. m. nom. sg.) followed; **dūram**– (ind.) far; **pitrā**– (m. n. inst. sg.) by His father; **daśarathena**– (m. n. inst. sg.) by King Daśaratha; **ca**– (ind.) also.

Prose order

rāmasya dayitā bhāryā nityaṁ prāṇa-samā hitā janakasya kule jātā deva-māyā iva nirmitā sarva-lakṣaṇa-sampannā nārīṇām uttamā

---

[18] The ruler of the kingdom of Videha.

[19] Rohiṇī is personified as the wife of the moon-god.

vadhūḥ sītā api śaśinaṁ rohiṇī yathā rāmam anugatā | pauraiḥ pitrā daśarathena ca dūram anugataḥ |

Translation

Śrī Rāma's beloved wife, Sītā, who is like His very life and is always affectionate to Him, also followed Him just as the constellation Rohiṇī follows the moon. Sītā appeared in the house of King Janaka and her form seems as beautiful as God's yoga-māyā. She is endowed with all auspicious characteristics and is indeed the best among all women. The citizens and His father, Daśaratha, also followed Him for a long distance.

श्री राम की प्रिय पत्नी सीता ने भी, जो उनके प्राण के समान हैं और हमेशा उनका हित करने वाली हैं, उनका अनुसरण किया, जैसे रोहिणी चन्द्रमा का अनुसरण करती है। सीता जी महाराज जनक के कुल में प्रकट हुई थीं और उनका रूप देवमाया की भांति सुन्दर है। वे सब शुभ लक्षणों से युक्त हैं और नारियों में उत्तम हैं। अयोध्या निवासी और महाराज दशरथ भी दूर तक श्री राम के पीछे गए।

TEXT 29

शृङ्गवेरपुरे सूतं गङ्गाकूले व्यसर्जयत् ।

गुहमासाद्य धर्मात्मा निषादाधिपतिं प्रियम् ॥ २९ ॥

śṛṅgavera-pure sūtaṁ gaṅgā-kūle vyasarjayat |

guham āsādya dharmātmā niṣādādhipatiṁ priyam || 29 ||

śṛṅgavera– (m. n.) named Śṛṅgavera; **pura**– (neu. n.) town; **śṛṅgavera-pure**– (tp. cp./neu. n. loc. sg.) in the town named Śṛṅgavera; **sūtam**– (m. n. acc. sg.) to the charioteer; **gaṅgā**– (f. n.) the river Ganges; **kūla**– (neu. n.) the bank; **gaṅgā-kūle**– (tp. cp. neu. loc. sg.) at the bank of the river Ganges; **vyasarjayat**– (vi + sarjay[20], imp. 3rd p. sg.) sent away; **guham**– (m. n. acc. sg.) to Guha; **āsādya**– (abs., ā + √ sad) having approached; **dharma**– (m. n.) religious principles; **ātman**– (m. n.) mind; **dharmātmā**– (bv. cp./m. adj. nom. sg.) he whose mind is on dharma, virtuous; **niṣāda**– (m. n.) an outcaste tribe; **adhipati**– (m. n.) the ruler; **niṣādādhipatim**– (tp. cp. m. acc. sg.) the ruler of the Niṣādas; **priyam**– (m. adj. acc. sg.) dear.

Prose order

gaṅgā-kūle śṛṅgavera-pure priyaṁ niṣādādhipatiṁ guham āsādya dharmātmā sūtaṁ vyasarjayat |

Translation

Having approached His dear friend Guha, the King of the Niṣādas, in the town called Śṛṅgavera, which is on the bank of the river Ganges, Śrī Rāma sent away His charioteer, Sumantra.

---

[20] Causative verbal form of the root *sṛj*.

गंगा के किनारे पर श्रृंगवेरपुर में अपने प्रिय मित्र निषादराज गुह के पास पहुँच कर धर्मात्मा राम ने अपने सारथी सुमंत्र को लौटा दिया।

TEXTS 30 - 31

गुहेन सहितो रामो लक्ष्मणेन च सीतया ।
ते वनेन वनं गत्वा नदीस्तीर्त्वा बहूदकाः ॥ ३० ॥
चित्रकूटमनुप्राप्य भरद्वाजस्य शासनात् ।
रम्यमावसथं कृत्वा रममाणा वने त्रयः ॥ ३१ ॥
देवगन्धर्वसङ्काशास्तत्र ते न्यवसन् सुखम् ।

guhena sahito rāmo lakṣmaṇena ca sītayā |

te vanena vanaṁ gatvā nadīs tīrtvā bahūdakāḥ || 30 ||

citrakūṭam anuprāpya bharadvājasya śāsanāt|

ramyam āvasathaṁ kṛtvā ramamāṇā vane trayaḥ || 31 ||

deva-gandharva-saṅkāśās tatra te nyavasan sukham |

guhena– (m. n. inst. sg.) by Guha; **sahitaḥ**– (m. adj. nom. sg.) accompanied ; **rāmaḥ**– (m. n. nom. sg.) Śrī Rāma; **lakṣmaṇena**– (m. n. inst. sg.) by Lakṣmaṇa; **ca**– (ind.) and; **sītayā**– (f. n. inst. sg.) by Sītā; **te**– (3rd p. pron. nom. m. pl.) they; **vanena**– (neu. n. inst. sg.) by forest; **vanam**– (neu. n. acc. sg.) to forest; **gatvā**– (abs., √gam) having gone; **nadīḥ**– (f. n. acc. pl.) rivers; **tīrtvā**–

(abs., √ tṝ) having crossed; **bahu**– (adj.) abundant; **udaka**– (neu. n.) water; **bahūdakāḥ**– (bv. cp./f. adj. acc. pl.) of abundant waters; **citrakūṭam**– (m. n. acc. sg.) the hill named Citrakūṭa; **anuprāpya**– (abs., anu + pra + √ āp) having reached; **bharadvājasya**– (m. n. gen. sg.) of the sage Bharadvāja; **śāsanāt**– (neu. n. abl. sg.) by the command; **ramyam**– (m. adj. acc. sg.) pleasant; **āvasatham**– (m. n. acc. sg.) hut; **kṛtvā**– (abs., √ kṛ) having built; **ramamāṇāḥ**– (√ ram, m. prp. nom. pl.) enjoying; **vane**– (neu. n. loc. sg.) in the forest; **trayaḥ**– (num. m. pl.) the three of them; **deva**– (m. n.) heavenly beings; **gandharva**– (m. n.) celestial musicians; **saṅkāśa**– (m. n.) appearing like; **deva-gandharva-saṅkāśāḥ**– (tp. cp./m. adj. nom. pl.) looking like celestial beings and Gandharvas; **tatra**– (ind.) there; **te**– (3rd p. pron. m. nom. pl.) they; **nyavasan**– (ni + √ vas, imp. 3rdp. pl.) resided; **sukham**– (ind.) happily.

Prose order

guhena lakṣmaṇena sītayā ca sahitaḥ rāmaḥ (āsīt) | te vanena vanaṁ gatvā bahūdakāḥ nadīḥ tīrtvā bharadvājasya śāsanāt citrakūṭam anuprāpya tatra ramyam āvasathaṁ kṛtvā vane deva-gandharva-saṅkāśāḥ ramamāṇāḥ te trayaḥ sukhaṁ nyavasan |

Translation

Accompanied by Guha, Lakṣmaṇa and Sītā, Śrī Rāma moved from forest to forest and crossed rivers of vast waters. Having reached the Citrakūṭa Hill by the direction of the sage

Bharadvāja, they built a hut and the three of them happily resided in the forest, enjoying like celestial beings and Gandharvas.

गुह, लक्ष्मण और सीता के साथ श्री राम वन से वन चलकर विशाल नदियाँ पार करके भरद्वाज मुनि के आदेश से चित्रकूट पहुँचे। उस वन में एक रम्य कुटीर बनाकर श्री राम, सीता तथा लक्ष्मण देवों और गन्धर्वों की तरह विहार करते हुए सुख से रहे।

TEXT 32

चित्रकूटं गते रामे पुत्रशोकातुरस्तदा ।
राजा दशरथः स्वर्गं जगाम विलपन् सुतम् ॥ ३२ ॥

citrakūṭaṁ gate rāme putra-śokāturas tadā |
rājā daśarathaḥ svargaṁ jagāma vilapan sutam || 32 ||

citrakūṭam– (m. n. acc. sg.) to Citrakūṭa; **gate**– (loc. abs., m. sg.) having gone; **rāme**– (loc. abs., m. sg.) Śrī Rāma; **putra**– (m. n.) son; **śoka**– (m. n.) grief; **ātura**– (adj.) afflicted; **putra-śokāturaḥ**– (tp. cp./m. adj. nom. sg.) afflicted by grief because of his son; **tadā**– (ind.) then; **rājā**– (m. n. nom. sg.) king; **daśarathaḥ**– (m. n. nom. sg.) Daśaratha; **svargam**– (m. n. acc. sg.) to heaven; **jagāma**– (√ gam, perf. 3rd p. sg.) went; **vilapan**– (vi + √ lap, m. prp. nom. sg.) bewailing; **sutam**– (m. n. acc. sg.) son.

Prose order

citrakūṭaṁ gate rāme sutaṁ vilapan putra-śokāturaḥ rājā daśarathaḥ tadā svargaṁ jagāma |

Translation

As Śrī Rāma left for Citrakūṭa, bewailing the loss of his son and afflicted because of Him, King Daśaratha went to heaven.

श्री राम के चित्रकूट जाने पर अपने पुत्र के कारण शोक पीड़ित महाराज दशरथ विलाप करते हुए स्वर्ग चले गए।

TEXTS 33 - 34

गते तु तस्मिन् भरतो वसिष्ठप्रमुखैर्द्विजैः ॥ ३३ ॥

नियुज्यमानो राज्याय नैच्छद्राज्यं महाबलः ।

स जगाम वनं वीरो रामपादप्रसादकः ॥ ३४ ॥

gate tu tasmin bharato vasiṣṭha-pramukhair dvijaiḥ || 33 ||

niyujyamāno rājyāya naicchad rājyaṁ mahā-balaḥ |

sa jagāma vanaṁ vīro rāma-pāda-prasādakaḥ || 34 ||

gate– (loc. abs., m. sg.) having departed from this world; **tu**– (ind.) then; **tasmin**– (loc. abs., m. sg.) he (the King); **bharataḥ**– (m. n. nom. sg.) Prince Bharata; **vasiṣṭha**– (m. n.) the sage

Vasiṣṭha; **pramukha**– (adj.) chief; **vasiṣṭha-pramukhaiḥ**– (bv. cp./m. adj. inst. pl.) headed by the sage Vasiṣṭha; **dvijaiḥ**– (m. n. inst. pl.) by the twice born brāhmaṇas; **niyujyamānaḥ**– (m. pr.pp. nom. sg.) being appointed; **rājyāya**– (neu. n. dat. sg.) for the kingdom; **na**– (ind.) not; **aicchat**– (√ iṣ, imp., 3rd p. sg.); **rājyam**– (neu. n. acc. sg.) the kingdom; **mahat**– (adj.) great; **bala**– (neu. n.) strength; **mahā-balaḥ**– (bv. cp./m. adj. nom. sg.) he whose strength is great; **saḥ**– (3rd p. pron. nom. m. sg.) he; **jagāma**– (√ gam, perf. 3rd p. sg.) went; **vanam**– (neu. n. acc. sg.) to the forest; **vīraḥ**– (m. n. nom. sg.) the hero; **rāma**– (m. n.) Śrī Rāma; **pāda**– (m. n.) the feet; **prasādaka**– (adj.) desiring to propitiate; **rāma-pāda-prasādakaḥ**– (tp. cp./m. adj. nom. sg.) desiring to propitiate Śrī Rāma's lotus feet.

Prose order

gate tu tasmin vasiṣṭha-pramukhaiḥ dvijaiḥ rājyāya niyujyamānaḥ bharataḥ rājyaṁ na aicchat | saḥ mahā-balaḥ vīraḥ rāma-pāda-prasādakaḥ vanaṁ jagāma |

Translation

When King Daśaratha passed away, the brāhmaṇas headed by the sage Vasiṣṭha appointed Bharata to rule the kingdom, but he did not want it. That hero of great power then departed for the forest with the desire to propitiate Śrī Rāma.

महाराज दशरथ के स्वर्गवास होने पर, राज्य शासन के लिए वसिष्ठ आदि ब्राह्मणों द्वारा भरत नियुक्त किये गये थे, परंतु उन्होंने राज्य को नहीं चाहा। तब श्री राम को प्रसन्न करने के इच्छुक वे बलवान वीर वन चले गये।

TEXT 35

गत्वा तु स महात्मानं रामं सत्यपराक्रमम् ।

अयाचद् भ्रातरं राममार्यभावपुरस्कृतः ॥ ३५ ॥

त्वमेव राजा धर्मज्ञ इति रामं वचोऽब्रवीत् ।

gatvā tu sa mahātmānaṁ rāmaṁ satya-parākramam |

ayācad bhrātaraṁ rāmam ārya-bhāva-puraskṛtaḥ || 35 ||

tvam eva rājā dharma-jña iti rāmaṁ vaco'bravīt |

gatvā– (abs., √ gam) having gone; **tu**– (ind.) then; **saḥ**– (3rd p. pron. nom. m. sg.) he; **mahat**– (adj.) great; **ātman**– (m. n.) soul; **mahātmānam**– (m. adj. acc. sg.) to the great soul; **rāmam**– (m. n. acc. sg.) to Śrī Rāma; **satya**– (adj.) real; **parākrama**– (m. n.) prowess; **satya-parākramam**– (bv. cp./m. adj. acc. sg.) to him whose prowess is real; **ayācat**– (√ yāc, imp. 3rdp. sg.) requested; **bhrātaram**– (m. n. acc. sg.) his brother; **rāmam**– (m. n. acc. sg.) to Śrī Rāma; **ārya**– (adj.) honourable; **bhāva**– (m. n.) behaviour; **puraskṛta**– (adj.) placing in front; **ārya-bhāva-puraskṛtaḥ**– (tp. cp./m. adj. nom. sg.) accompanied by a honourable behaviour; **tvam**– (2nd p. pron. nom. sg.) You; **eva**– (ind.) only; **rājā**– (m. n.

nom. sg.) king; **dharma**– (m. n.) religious principles; **jña**– (adj.) knower; **dharma-jñaḥ**– (tp. cp./m. adj. nom. sg.) knower of dharma; **iti**– (ind.) thus; **rāmam**– (m. n. acc. sg.) to Śrī Rāma; **vacaḥ**– (neu. n. acc. sg.) speech; **abravīt**– (√ brū, imp. 3rd p. sg.) spoke.

Prose order

ārya-bhāva-puraskṛtaḥ saḥ tu satya-parākramaṁ mahātmānaṁ rāmaṁ gatvā bhrātaraṁ rāmam ayācat tvam eva dharma-jñaḥ rājā iti rāmaṁ vacaḥ abravīt |

Translation

Exhibiting very respectable behaviour, Bharata went to his brother, the high-souled and truly heroic Rāma, and spoke the following words: "Only you are the King, the knower of dharma."

तब आदरभाव से युक्त भरत अपने पराक्रमी धर्मात्मा भाई श्री राम के पास जाकर यह वचन बोले — "आप ही धर्मज्ञ राजा हैं"।

TEXTS 36 - 37

रामोऽपि परमोदारः सुमुखः सुमहायशाः ॥ ३६ ॥

न चैच्छत् पितुरादेशाद्राज्यं रामो महाबलः ।

पादुके चास्य राज्याय न्यासं दत्त्वा पुनः पुनः ॥ ३७ ॥

निवर्तयामास ततो भरतं भरताग्रजः ।

rāmo'pi paramodāraḥ sumukhaḥ sumahā-yaśāḥ || 36 ||

na caicchat pitur ādeśād rājyaṁ rāmo mahā-balaḥ |

pāduke cāsya rājyāya nyāsaṁ dattvā punaḥ punaḥ || 37 ||

nivartayām āsa tato bharataṁ bharatāgrajaḥ |

rāmaḥ– (m. n. nom. sg.) Śrī Rāma; **api**– (ind.) also; **parama**– (adj.) best; **udāra**– (adj.) munificent; **paramodāraḥ**– (tp. cp./m. adj. nom. sg.) the best of the munificent ones; **su-mukhaḥ**– (m. adj. nom. sg.) handsome; **su-mahat**– (adj.) very great; **yaśas**– (neu. n.) fame; **su-mahā-yaśāḥ**– (bv. cp./m. adj. nom. sg.) he whose fame is very great; **na**– (ind.) not; **ca**– (ind.) and; **aicchat**– (√ iṣ, imp. 3rd p. sg.) desired; **pituḥ**– (m. n. gen. sg.) of the father; **ādeśāt**– (m. n. abl. sg.) due to the command; **rājyam**– (neu. n. acc. sg.) the kingdom; **rāmaḥ**– (m. n. nom. sg.) Śrī Rāma; **mahat**– (adj.) great; **bala**– (m. n.) strength; **mahā-balaḥ**– (bv. cp./ m. adj. nom. sg.) he whose strength is very great; **pāduke**– (neu. n. acc. du.) the sandals; **ca**– (ind.) and; **asya**– (d. pron. m. gen. sg.) for him (Bharata); **rājyāya**– (neu. n. dat. sg.) for the kingdom; **nyāsam**– (m. n. acc. sg.) pledge; **dattvā**– (abs., √ dā) having given; **punaḥ punaḥ**– (ind.) again and again; **nivartayām āsa**– (ni + vartay[21], perf. 3rd p. sg.) made him return; **tataḥ**– (ind.) then; **bharatam**– (m. n. acc. sg.) to Bharata; **agraja**– (adj.) born before;

[21] This is the causative verbal form of the root *vṛ*.

bharatāgrajaḥ– (tp. cp./m. adj. nom. sg.) the elder brother of Bharata.

Prose order

paramodāraḥ sumukhaḥ sumahā-yaśāḥ rāmaḥ ca api pituḥ ādeśāt rājyaṁ na aicchat | tataḥ ca mahā-balaḥ bharatāgrajaḥ rāmaḥ rājyāya asya pāduke nyāsaṁ dattvā punaḥ punaḥ bharataṁ nivartayām āsa |

Translation

Due to His father's command, Śrī Rāma, Who is highly munificent, very handsome and glorious, did not desire the kingdom. The greatly powerful Rāma, the elder brother of Bharata, then gave His wooden sandals to Bharata as a pledge for the kingdom and insisted repeatedly that he should return.

अपने पिता के आदेश के कारण परम उदार सुमुख महायशस्वी श्री राम ने राज्य को नहीं चाहा । तब भरताग्रज श्री राम ने प्रतिनिधि के रूप में अपनी पादुका देकर बार बार उनको लौटने को कहा ।

TEXT 38

स काममनवाप्यैव रामपादावुपस्पृशन् ॥ ३८ ॥
नन्दिग्रामेऽकरोद्राज्यं रामागमनकाङ्क्षया ।

sa kāmam anavāpyaiva rāma-pādāv upaspṛśan || 38 ||

nandigrāme'karod rājyaṁ rāmāgamana-kāṅkṣayā |

saḥ– (3rd p. pron. nom. m. sg.) he; **kāmam**– (m. n. acc. sg.) wish; **anavāpya**– (abs., an + ava + √ āp) not having obtained; **eva**– (ind.) indeed; **rāma**– (m. n.) Śrī Rāma; **pāda**– (m. n.) foot; **rāma-pādau**– (tp. cp./m. n. acc. du.) Śrī Rāma's feet; **upaspṛśan**– (upa + √ spṛś, m. prp. nom. sg.) touching; **nandigrāme**– (m. n. loc. sg.) at the place called Nandigrāma; **akarot**– (√ kṛ, imp. 3rd p. sg.) executed; **rājyam**– (neu. n. acc. sg.) the kingdom; **rāma**– (m. n.) Śrī Rāma; **āgamana**– (neu. n.) return; **kāṅkṣā**– (f. n.) desire; **rāmāgamana-kāṅkṣayā**– (tp.cp. f. inst. sg.) with the desire for Śrī Rāma's return.

Prose order

saḥ kāmam anavāpya eva nandigrāme rāma-pādau upaspṛśan rāmāgamana-kāṅkṣayā rājyam akarot |

Translation

Not having attained his wish, Bharata went to Nandigrāma,[22] where he ruled the kingdom while constantly revering Śrī Rāma's feet with the desire that He would return.

---

[22] Failing to convince Śrī Rāma to return to Ayodhyā, Bharata also refused to return, but to abide by His order, he ruled as His representative from a nearby village where he spent fourteen years living like an ascetic.

अपनी कामना अपूर्ण होने पर भरत ने नन्दिग्राम जाकर, श्री राम के आगमन की प्रतीक्षा करते हुए और उनकी पादुकाओं को प्रणाम करते हुए राज्य शासन किया।

Araṇya-kāṇḍa

TEXTS 39 - 40

गते तु भरते श्रीमान् सत्यसंधो जितेन्द्रियः ॥ ३९ ॥

रामस्तु पुनरालक्ष्य नागरस्य जनस्य च ।

तत्रागमनमेकाग्रो दण्डकान् प्रविवेश ह ॥ ४० ॥

gate tu bharate śrīmān satya-saṁdho jitendriyaḥ || 39 ||

rāmas tu punar ālakṣya nāgarasya janasya ca |

tatrāgamanam ekāgro daṇḍakān praviveśa ha || 40 ||

gate– (loc. abs. m. sg.) having gone; **tu**– (ind.) then; **bharate**– (loc. abs. m. sg.) Bharata; **śrī**– (f. n.) fortune; **mat**– (adj. aff.) possessing; **śrīmān**– (m. adj. nom. sg.) fortunate; **satya**– (adj.) true; **saṁdhā**– (f. n.) promise; **satya-saṁdhaḥ**– (bv. cp./m. adj. nom. sg.) he who is true to his promise; **jita**– (ppp./adj.) conquered; **indriya**– (neu. n.) sense; **jitendriyaḥ**– (bv. cp./m. adj.

nom. sg.) he whose senses are controlled; **rāmaḥ**– (m. n. nom. sg.) Śrī Rāma; **tu**– (ind.) then; **punaḥ**– (ind.) again; **ālakṣya**– (abs., ā + √ lakṣ) having seen the possibility; **nāgarasya**– (m. n. gen. sg.) of the citizens; **janasya**– (m. n. gen. sg.) of the people; **ca**– (ind.) and; **tatra**– (ind.) there; **āgamanam**– (neu. n. acc. sg.) coming; **ekāgraḥ**– (m. adj. nom. sg.) with a fixed mind; **daṇḍakān**– (m. n. acc. pl.) the forest called Daṇḍaka; **praviveśa**– (pra + √ viś, per. 3rd p. sg.) entered; **ha**– (ind.) indeed.

Prose order

gate tu bharate śrīmān satya-saṁdhaḥ jitendriyaḥ ekāgraḥ rāmaḥ tu nāgarasya janasya ca tatra punaḥ āgamanam ālakṣya daṇḍakān praviveśa ha |

Translation

After Bharata departed, seeing the possibility that the residents of Ayodhyā might come again, Śrī Rāma, Who is fortunate, true to His promises, of conquered senses and fixed mind, entered the Daṇḍaka forest.

भरत के जाने पर अयोध्या के नागरिक लोगों के फिर आने की संभावना देखकर श्रीमान् सत्यप्रतिज्ञ जितेन्द्रिय राम ने एकाग्र होकर दंडकारण्य में प्रवेश किया।

TEXT 41

प्रविश्य तु महारण्यं रामो राजीवलोचनः ।

विराधं राक्षसं हत्वा शरभङ्गं ददर्श ह ॥ ४१ ॥

सुतीक्ष्णं चाप्यगस्त्यं च अगस्त्यभ्रातरं तथा ।

pravिśya tu mahāraṇyaṁ rāmo rājīva-locanaḥ |

virādhaṁ rākṣasaṁ hatvā śarabhaṅgaṁ dadarśa ha || 41 ||

sutīkṣṇaṁ cāpy agastyaṁ ca agastya-bhrātaraṁ tathā |[23]

praviśya– (abs., pra + √ viś) having entered; **tu**– (ind.) then; **mahat**– (adj.) great; **araṇya**– (neu. n.) forest; **mahāraṇyam**– (tp. cp./neu. n. acc. sg.) great forest; **rāmaḥ**– (m. n. nom. sg.) Śrī Rāma; **rājīva**– (neu. nom.) blue lotus; **locana**– (neu. n.) eye; **rājīva-locanaḥ**– (bv. cp./m. adj. nom. sg.) he whose eyes are like blue lotuses; **virādham**– (m. n. acc. sg.) named Virādha; **rākṣasam**– (m. n. acc. sg.) a *rākṣasa*[24]; **hatvā**– (abs., √ han) having killed; **śarabhaṅgam**– (m. n. acc. sg.) the sage Śarabhaṅga; **dadarśa**– (√ dṛś, perf. 3rd p. sg.) saw; **ha**– (ind.) indeed; **sutīkṣṇam**– (m. n. acc. sg.) the sage Sutīkṣṇa; **ca**– (ind.) and; **api**– (ind.) also; **agastyam**– (m. n. acc. sg.) the sage Agastya; **ca**– (ind.) and; **agastya-bhrātaram**– (tp. cp. m. acc. sg.) Agastya's brother[25]; **tathā**– (ind.) as well.

---

[23] *Saṁdhi* is not compulsory between the *padas* (quarters) of a verse, therefore here we see 'ca agastya' instead of 'cāgastya.'

[24] A kind of devil.

[25] According to Govindarāja's commentary named *Rāmāyaṇa-bhūṣaṇa*, Sudarśana is the brother of Agastya referred to here.

Prose order

rājīva-locanaḥ rāmaḥ tu mahāraṇyaṁ praviśya virādhaṁ rākṣasaṁ hatvā śarabhaṅgaṁ sutīkṣṇaṁ ca api agastyaṁ ca agastya-bhrātaraṁ tathā dadarśa ha |

Translation

Having entered that great forest, lotus-eyed Rāma killed a rākṣasa named Virādha and saw the sages Śarabhaṅga, Sutīkṣṇa, Agastya and Agastya's brother.

उस महारण्य में प्रवेश करके राजीव लोचन श्री राम ने विराध नामक राक्षस का वध किया और शरभंग, सुतीक्ष्ण, अगस्त्य तथा अगस्त्य के भाई — इन सब मुनियों को देखा।

TEXT 42

अगस्त्यवचनाच्चैव जग्राहैन्द्रं शरासनम् ॥ ४२ ॥

खड्गं च परमप्रीतस्तूणी चाक्षयसायकौ ।

agastya-vacanāc caiva jagrāhaindraṁ śarāsanam || 42 ||

khaḍgaṁ ca parama-prītas tūṇī cākṣaya-sāyakau |

agastya– (m. n.) of Agastya; **vacana–** (neu. n.) word; **agastya-vacanāt–** (tp. cp./neu. abl. sg.) according to Agastya Muni's instruction; **ca–** (ind.) and; **eva–** (ind.) certainly; **jagrāha–** (√

grah, perf. 3rd p. sg.) obtained; **aindram**– (neu. adj. acc. sg.) belonging to Indra; **śara**– (m. n.) arrow; **āsana**– (neu. n.) seat; **śarāsanam**– (tp. cp./m. n. acc. sg.) bow; **khaḍgam**– (m. n. acc. sg.) sword; **ca**– (ind.) and; **parama**– (adj.) highest; **prīta**– (adj.) pleased; **parama-prītaḥ**– (tp. cp./m. adj. nom. sg.) very much pleased; **tūṇī**– (m. n. acc. du.) two quivers; **ca**– (ind.) and; **akṣaya**– (adj.) inexhaustible; **sāyaka**– (m. n.) arrow; **akṣaya-sāyakau**– (bv. cp./m. adj. acc. du.) whose arrows are inexhaustible.

Prose order

agastya-vacanāt parama-prītaḥ aindraṁ śarāsanaṁ ca khaḍgaṁ ca akṣaya-sāyakau tūṇī ca eva jagrāha |

Translation

Following Agastya Muni's instructions, Śrī Rāma obtained a bow that belonged to Indra, as well as a sword and a couple of quivers with inexhaustible arrows, and thus became very pleased.

अगस्त्य मुनि के वचन से श्री राम ने इंद्र के धनुष, तलवार तथा दो अक्षय बाण वाले तरकश ग्रहण किये और बहुत प्रसन्न हो गए।

TEXTS 43 - 44

वसतस्तस्य रामस्य वने वनचरैः सह ॥ ४३ ॥

ऋषयोऽभ्यागमन् सर्वे वधायासुररक्षसाम् ।

स तेषां प्रतिशुश्राव राक्षसानां तदा वने ॥ ४४ ॥

vasatas tasya rāmasya vane vana-caraiḥ saha || 43 ||

ṛṣayo'bhyāgaman sarve vadhāyāsura-rakṣasām |

sa teṣāṁ pratiśuśrāva rākṣasānāṁ tadā vane || 44 ||

vasataḥ– (√ vas, m. prp. gen. sg.) while residing; **tasya**– (3rd p. pron. gen. m. sg.) His; **rāmasya**– (m. n. gen. sg.) of Śrī Rāma; **vane**– (neu. n. loc. sg.) in the forest; **vana**– (neu. n.) forest; **cara**– (adj.) moving; **vana-caraiḥ**– (tp. cp. m. inst. pl.) with those who live in the forest; **saha**– (ind.) together with; **ṛṣayaḥ**– (m. n. nom. pl.) sages; **abhyāgaman**– (abhi + ā + √ gam, imp. 3rd p. pl.) approached; **sarve**– (adj. pron. m. nom. pl.) all; **vadhāya**– (m. n. dat. sg.) for killing; **asura-rakṣasām**– (dv. cp./gen. pl) of *asuras* and *rākṣasas*; **saḥ**– (3rd p. pron. nom. m. sg.) He; **teṣām**– (3rd p. pron. gen. m. pl.) to them; **pratiśuśrāva**– (prati + √ śru, per. 3rd p. sg.) assured; **rākṣasānām**– (m. n. gen. pl.) of the demons; **tadā**– (ind.) then; **vane**– (neu. n. loc. sg.) in the forest.

Prose order

vane vasataḥ tasya rāmasya sarve ṛṣayaḥ vana-caraiḥ saha asura-rakṣasāṁ vadhāya abhyāgaman | tadā saḥ vane rākṣasānāṁ (vadham) teṣāṁ pratiśuśrāva |

Translation

While Śrī Rāma was living in the forest, all the sages accompanied by other residents of that forest approached Him to request that He kill the asuras and rākṣasas there, and He assured them that these demons would be exterminated.

जब श्री राम वन में निवास कर रहे थे, सब ऋषि गण वन के दूसरे निवासियों के साथ उनके पास निवेदन करने गए कि "आप असुरों और राक्षसों का वध कीजिए"। तब उन्होंने उनके वध की प्रतिज्ञा की।

TEXT 45

प्रतिज्ञातश्च रामेण वधः संयति रक्षसाम् ।

ऋषीणामग्निकल्पानां दण्डकारण्यवासिनाम् ॥ ४५ ॥

pratijñātaś ca rāmeṇa vadhaḥ saṁyati rakṣasām |

ṛṣīṇām agni-kalpānāṁ daṇḍakāraṇya-vāsinām || 45 ||

pratijñātaḥ– (ppp. m. nom. sg.) promised; **ca**– (ind.) indeed; **rāmeṇa**– (m. n. inst. sg.) by Śrī Rāma; **vadhaḥ**– (m. n. nom. sg.) killing; **saṁyati**– (m. n. loc. sg.) in the battle; **rakṣasām**– (m. n. gen. pl.) of the demons; **ṛṣīṇām**– (m. n. gen. pl.) to the sages; **agni**– (m. n.) fire; **kalpa**– (adj.) similar to; **agni-kalpānām**– (tp. cp./m. adj. gen. pl.) to them who are like fire; **daṇḍakāraṇya**– (neu. n.) the Daṇḍaka forest; **vāsin**– (adj.) inhabiting;

daṇḍakāraṇya-vāsinām– (tp. cp./m. adj. gen. pl.) to them who inhabited the Daṇḍaka forest.

Prose order

agni-kalpānāṁ daṇḍakāraṇya-vāsinām ṛṣīṇāṁ rāmeṇa saṁyati rakṣasāṁ vadhaḥ pratijñātaḥ ca |

Translation

Indeed, Śrī Rāma promised those fire-like effulgent sages who lived in the Daṇḍaka forest that He would kill the demons in the battle.

श्री राम ने उन अग्नि के सदृश तेजस्वी दंडकारण्य निवासी ऋषिओं से युद्ध में राक्षसों के वध की प्रतिज्ञा की।

TEXT 46

तेन तत्रैव वसता जनस्थाननिवासिनी ।

विरूपिता शूर्पणखा राक्षसी कामरूपिणी ॥ ४६ ॥

tena tatraiva vasatā janasthāna-nivāsinī |

virūpitā śūrpaṇakhā rākṣasī kāma-rūpiṇī || 46 ||

tena– (3rd p. pron. m. inst. sg.) by Him; **tatra**– (ind.) there; **eva**– (ind.) indeed; **vasatā**– (√ vas, m. prp. inst. sg.) residing; **janasthāna**– (neu. n.) the place called Janasthāna; **nivāsin**– (adj.) resident; **janasthāna-nivāsinī**– (tp. cp./f. adj. nom. sg.) resident of Janasthāna; **virūpitā**– (ppp./f. adj. nom. sg.) disfigured; **śūrpaṇakhā**– (f. n. nom. sg.) named Śūrpaṇakhā; **rākṣasī**– (f. n. nom. sg.) a demoness; **kāma**– (m. n.) wish; **rūpin**– (adj.) having a form; **kāma-rūpiṇī**– (bv. cp./f. adj. nom. sg.) assuming a form at her will.

Prose order

tatra eva vasatā tena janasthāna-nivāsinī kāma-rūpiṇī rākṣasī śūrpaṇakhā virūpitā (kāritā)[26]|

Translation

While Śrī Rāma was living there, by His order Śūrpaṇakhā, a demoness who resided at Janasthāna and was able to assume any form at her will, was disfigured by Lakṣmaṇa.

वहाँ निवास करते हुए श्री राम की आज्ञा से जनस्थान की रहने वाली कामरूपिणी शूर्पणखा नामक एक राक्षसी लक्ष्मण द्वारा विकृत की गई।

[26] There is an implied causative action here: Rāma caused Śūrpaṇakhā to be disfigured by Lakṣmaṇa.

TEXT 47

ततः शूर्पणखावाक्यादुद्युक्तान् सर्वराक्षसान् ।

खरं त्रिशिरसं चैव दूषणं चैव राक्षसम् ॥ ४७ ॥

निजघान रणे रामस्तेषां चैव पदानुगान् ।

tataḥ śūrpaṇakhā-vākyād udyuktān sarva-rākṣasān |

kharaṁ triśirasaṁ caiva dūṣaṇaṁ caiva rākṣasam || 47 ||

nijaghāna raṇe rāmas teṣāṁ caiva padānugān |

tataḥ– (ind.) then; **śūrpaṇakhā**– (f. n.) the demoness Śūrpaṇakhā; **vākya**– (neu. n.) word; **śūrpaṇakhā-vākyāt**– (tp. cp./neu. abl. sg.) on account of Śūrpaṇakhā's words; **udyuktān**– (ppp./m. adj. acc. pl.) incited; **sarva**– (adj. pron.) all; **rākṣasa**– (m. n.) demon; **sarva-rākṣasān**– (tp. cp. m. acc. pl.) to all the demons; **kharam**– (m. n. acc. sg.) to Khara; **triśirasam**– (m. n. acc. sg.) to Triśirā; **ca**– (ind.) and; **eva**– (ind.) indeed; **dūṣaṇam**– (m. n. acc. sg.) to Dūṣaṇa; **ca**– (ind.) and; **eva**– (ind.) indeed; **rākṣasam**– (m. n. acc. sg.) to the demon; **nijaghāna**– (√ han, perf. 3rd p. sg.) killed; **raṇe**– (m. n. loc. sg.) in the battle; **rāmaḥ**– (m. n. nom. sg.) Śrī Rāma; **teṣām**– (3rd p. pron. m. gen. pl.) their; **ca**– (ind.) and; **eva**– (ind.) indeed; **pada**– (neu. n.) step; **anuga**– (adj.) follower; **padānugān**– (tp. cp./m. adj. acc. pl.) companions.

Prose order

tataḥ raṇe rāmaḥ śūrpaṇakhā-vākyāt udyuktān sarva-rākṣasān kharaṁ triśirasaṁ ca eva dūṣaṇaṁ rākṣasaṁ ca eva teṣāṁ padānugān ca eva nijaghāna |

Translation

Then in battle, Śrī Rāma killed all those rākṣasas, including Khara, Triśirā, Dūṣaṇa and their companions, who had been instigated by Śūrpaṇakhā's words.

तब युद्ध में श्री राम ने शूर्पणखा के वचन से प्रेरित खर, त्रिशिरा, दूषण और उनके अनुयायी राक्षसों का वध किया।

TEXT 48

वने तस्मिन् निवसता जनस्थाननिवासिनाम् ॥ ४८ ॥

रक्षसां निहतान्यासन् सहस्राणि चतुर्दश ।

vane tasmin nivasatā janasthāna-nivāsinām || 48 ||

rakṣasāṁ nihatāny āsan sahasrāṇi catur-daśa |

vane– (neu. n. loc. sg.) in the forest; **tasmin**– (3rd p. pron. neu. loc. sg.) in that; **nivasatā**– (ni + √vas, m. prp. inst. sg.) residing; **janasthāna**– (neu. n.) the place called Janasthāna; **nivāsin**– (adj.) residing; **janasthāna-nivāsinām**– (tp. cp./m. adj. gen. pl.)

residing at Janasthāna; **rakṣasām**– (m. n. gen. pl.) of the demons; **nihatāni**– (ppp. neu. nom. pl.) killed; **āsan**– (√ as, imp. 3rd p. pl.) were; **sahasrāṇi**– (neu. num. nom. pl.) thousands; **catur-daśa**– (num. nom. pl.) fourteen.

Prose order

tasmin vane nivasatā janasthāna-nivāsināṁ rakṣasāṁ catur-daśa sahasrāṇi nihatāni āsan |

Translation

While living in the Daṇḍaka forest, fourteen thousand rākṣasa residents of Janasthāna were killed by Śrī Rāma.

दंडकारण्य में रहते हुए श्री राम द्वारा चौदह हजार जनस्थान के रहने वाले राक्षस मारे गए।

TEXT 49

ततो ज्ञातिवधं श्रुत्वा रावणः क्रोधमूर्छितः ॥ ४९ ॥

सहायं वरयामास मारीचं नाम राक्षसम् ।

tato jñāti-vadhaṁ śrutvā rāvaṇaḥ krodha-mūrchitaḥ || 49 ||

sahāyaṁ varayām āsa mārīcaṁ nāma rākṣasam |

tataḥ– (ind.) then; **jñāti**– (m. n.) kinsmen; **vadha**– (m. n.) killing; **jñāti-vadham**– (tp. cp. m. acc. sg.) the killing of his kinsmen; **śrutvā**– (abs., √ śru) having heard; **rāvaṇaḥ**– (m. n. nom. sg.) Rāvaṇa, the King of the *rākṣasas;* **krodha**– (m. n.) anger; **mūrchita**– (ppp./adj.) agitated; **krodha-mūrchitaḥ**– (tp. cp./m. adj. nom. sg.) agitated by anger; **sahāyam**– (m. n. acc. sg.) assistant; **varayām āsa**– (√ vṛ, per. 3rd p. sg.) requested; **mārīcam**– (m. n. acc. sg.) Mārīca; **nāma**– (ind.) named; **rākṣasam**– (m. n. acc. sg.) a demon.

Prose order

tataḥ jñāti-vadhaṁ śrutvā krodha-mūrchitaḥ rāvaṇaḥ mārīcaṁ nāma rākṣasaṁ sahāyaṁ varayām āsa |

Translation

After that, having heard that his kinsmen had been killed, Rāvaṇa, the King of the rākṣasas, requested the help of a rākṣasa named Mārīca.

तत्पश्चात् अपने परिवार का वध सुनकर राक्षसराज रावण ने मारीच नामक एक राक्षस से सहायता माँगी।

TEXTS 50 - 51

वार्यमाणः सुबहुशो मारीचेन स रावणः ॥ ५० ॥

न विरोधो बलवता क्षमो रावण तेन ते ।

अनादृत्य तु तद्वाक्यं रावणः कालचोदितः ॥ ५१ ॥

जगाम सहमारीचस्तस्याश्रमपदं तदा ।

vāryamāṇaḥ su-bahuśo mārīcena sa rāvaṇaḥ || 50 ||

na virodho balavatā kṣamo rāvaṇa tena te |

anādṛtya tu tad-vākyaṁ rāvaṇaḥ kāla-coditaḥ || 51 ||

jagāma saha-mārīcas tasyāśrama-padaṁ tadā |

vāryamāṇaḥ– (vāray[27], m. pr.pp. nom. sg.) being prevented; **su-bahuśaḥ**– (ind.) repeatedly; **mārīcena**– (m. n. inst. sg.) by Mārīca; **saḥ**– (3rd p. pron. m. nom. sg.) he; **rāvaṇaḥ**– (m. n. nom. sg.) King Rāvaṇa; **na**– (ind.) not; **virodhaḥ**– (m. n. nom. sg.) strife; **bala**– (neu. n.) strength; **vat**– (adj. aff.) possessing; **balavatā**– (m. adj. inst. sg.) with the powerful; **kṣamaḥ**– (m. adj. nom. sg.) appropriate; **rāvaṇa**– (m. n. voc. sg.) O Rāvaṇa; **tena**– (3rd p. pron. m. inst. sg.) with Him; **te**– (2nd p. pron. gen. sg.) yours; **anādṛtya**– (ind.) ignoring; **tu**– (ind.) however; **tat**– (p. pron.) of his; **vākya**– (neu. n.) speech; **tad-vākyam**– (tp. cp. neu. acc. sg.) his words; **rāvaṇaḥ**– (m. n. nom. sg.) King Rāvaṇa; **kāla**– (m. n.) death in the form of time; **codita**– (ppp./adj.) impelled; **kāla-coditaḥ**– (tp. cp./m. adj. nom. sg.) being impelled by time; **jagāma**– (√ gam, per. 3rd p. sg.) went; **saha**– (ind.) together;

[27] This is the causative verbal form of the root *vṛ*.

saha-mārīcaḥ– (bv. cp./m. adj. nom. sg.) together with Mārīca; **tasya**– (3rd p. pron. m. gen. sg.) His; **āśrama-padam**– (neu. n. acc. sg.) hermitage; **tadā**– (ind.) then.

Prose order

"rāvaṇa, balavatā tena te virodhaḥ na kṣamaḥ" (iti) saḥ rāvaṇaḥ su-bahuśaḥ mārīcena vāryamāṇaḥ | kāla-coditaḥ rāvaṇaḥ tu tad-vākyam anādṛtya tadā saha-mārīcaḥ tasya āśrama-padaṁ jagāma |

Translation

"O Rāvaṇa, it is inappropriate that you should fight with that powerful hero." Rāvaṇa was thus repeatedly deflected by Mārīca. However, being impelled by the force of time, ignoring his words, Rāvaṇa then went to Śrī Rāma's hermitage with Mārīca.

"हे रावण, उस शक्तिशाली वीर से विरोध करना आपके लिए उचित नहीं है" — इस प्रकार मारीच ने बार बार रावण को मना किया, लेकिन काल से प्रेरित रावण उसकी बात न माना और मारीच के साथ श्री राम के आश्रम चला गया।

TEXT 52

तेन मायाविना दूरमपवाह्य नृपात्मजौ ॥ ५२ ॥

जहार भार्यां रामस्य गृध्रं हत्वा जटायुषम् ।

tena māyāvinā dūram apavāhya nṛpātmajau || 52 ||

jahāra bhāryāṁ rāmasya gṛdhraṁ hatvā jaṭāyuṣam |

tena– (3rd p. pron. m. inst. sg.) by him; **māyā**– (f. n.) illusion; **vin**– (adj. aff.) possessing; **māyāvinā**– (m. adj. inst. sg.) possessing magical powers; **dūram**– (ind.) far; **apavāhya**– (abs., apa + vāhay[28]) having caused them to be taken away; **nṛpa**– (m. n.) king; **ātman**– (m. n.) self; **ja**– (adj.) born from; **nṛpātmajau**– (tp. cp. m. acc. du.) the two sons of the King; **jahāra**– (√ hṛ, per. 3rd p. sg.) carried away; **bhāryām**– (f. n. acc. sg.) the wife; **rāmasya**– (m. n. gen. sg.) of Śrī Rāma; **gṛdhram**– (m. n. acc. sg.) the vulture; **hatvā**– (abs., √ han) having defeated; **jaṭāyuṣam**– (m. n. acc. sg.) named Jaṭāyu.

Prose order

māyāvinā tena nṛpātmajau dūram apavāhya gṛdhraṁ jaṭāyuṣaṁ hatvā rāmasya bhāryāṁ jahāra |

Translation

Having made the illusionist Mārīca take the two princes far away, Rāvaṇa took Śrī Rāma's wife, Sītā, after defeating Jaṭāyu, the King of vultures.

मायावी मारीच के द्वारा दोनों राजकुमारों को दूर तक गुमराह कर रावण ने गिद्धराज जटायु को मारकर श्री राम की पत्नी सीता का हरण किया।

---

[28] This is the causative verbal form of the root *vah*.

TEXT 53

गृध्रं च निहतं दृष्ट्वा हृतां श्रुत्वा च मैथिलीम् ॥ ५३ ॥

राघवः शोकसंतप्तो विललापाकुलेन्द्रियः ।

gṛdhraṁ ca nihataṁ dṛṣṭvā hṛtāṁ śrutvā ca maithilīm || 53 ||

rāghavaḥ śoka-saṁtapto vilalāpākulendriyaḥ |

gṛdhram– (m. n. acc. sg.) the vulture Jaṭāyu; **ca**– (ind.) and; **nihatam**– (ppp. m. acc. sg.) nearly killed; **dṛṣṭvā**– (abs., √ dṛś) having seen; **hṛtām**– (ppp. f. acc. sg.) taken away; **śrutvā**– (abs., √ śru) having heard; **ca**– (ind.) and; **maithilīm**– (f. n. acc. sg.) Sītā, the daughter of the King of Mithilā; **rāghavaḥ**– (m. n. nom. sg.) Śrī Rāma, the descendent of King Raghu; **śoka**– (m. n.) grief; **saṁtapta**– (ppp./adj.) afflicted; **śoka-saṁtaptaḥ**– (tp. cp./m. adj. nom. sg.) afflicted with grief; **vilalāpa**– (√ lap, per. 3rd p. sg.) lamented; **ākula**– (adj.) perturbed; **indriya**– (neu. n.) sense; **ākulendriyaḥ**– (bv. cp./m. adj. nom. sg.) he whose senses are perturbed.

Prose order

gṛdhraṁ ca nihataṁ dṛṣṭvā maithilīṁ ca hṛtāṁ śrutvā śoka-saṁtaptaḥ ākulendriyaḥ rāghavaḥ vilalāpa |

Translation

Seeing that the vulture Jaṭāyu was almost dead and hearing from him that Sītā was kidnapped, Śrī Rāma became afflicted with grief and lamented, His senses full of distress.

मृतप्रायः जटायु को देखकर और उसी से सीता का हरण सुनकर, शोकाकुल होकर व्याकुल इन्द्रियों से श्री राम ने विलाप किया।

TEXTS 54 - 55

ततस्तेनैव शोकेन गृध्रं दग्ध्वा जटायुषम् ॥ ५४ ॥

मार्गमाणो वने सीतां राक्षसं संददर्श ह ।

कबन्धं नाम रूपेण विकृतं घोरदर्शनम् ॥ ५५ ॥

tatas tenaiva śokena gṛdhraṁ dagdhvā jaṭāyuṣam || 54 ||

mārgamāṇo vane sītāṁ rākṣasaṁ saṁdadarśa ha |

kabandhaṁ nāma rūpeṇa vikṛtaṁ ghora-darśanam || 55 ||

tataḥ– (ind.) after that; **tena**– (3rd p. pron. neu. inst. sg.) by that; **eva**– (ind.) indeed; **śokena**– (m. n. inst. sg.) with grief; **gṛdhram**– (m. n. acc. sg.) the vulture; **dagdhvā**– (abs., √dah) having burnt; **jaṭāyuṣam**– (m. n. acc. sg.) Jaṭāyu; **mārgamāṇaḥ**– (√ mārg, m. prp. nom. sg.) searching; **vane**– (neu. n. loc. sg.) in the forest; **sītām**– (f. n. acc. sg.) Sītā; **rākṣasam**– (m. n. acc. sg.) a demon; **saṁdadarśa**– (sam + √dṛś, perf. 3rd p. sg.) saw; **ha**– (ind.) indeed; **kabandham**– (m. n. acc. sg.) Kabandha; **nāma**– (ind.) named;

rūpeṇa– (neu. n. inst. sg.) with a form; **vikṛtam**– (ppp./m. adj. acc. sg.) disfigured; **ghora**– (adj.) ghastly; **darśana**– (neu. n.) appearance; **ghora-darśanam**– (bv. cp./m. adj. acc. sg.) to him whose appearance is ghastly.

Prose order

tataḥ tena eva śokena jaṭāyuṣaṁ gṛdhraṁ dagdhvā vane sītāṁ mārgamāṇaḥ rūpeṇa vikṛtaṁ ghora-darśanaṁ kabandhaṁ nāma rākṣasaṁ saṁdadarśa ha |

Translation

Śrī Rāma Himself then burnt the body of Jaṭāyu with sorrow and while searching for Sītā in the forest, He saw a rākṣasa named Kabandha, who had a disfigured form and looked ghastly.

तत्पश्चात् शोक से श्री राम ने स्वयं जटायु का दाह संस्कार किया और वन में सीता को खोजते हुए विकृत रूप वाले घोर दर्शन कबंध नामक राक्षस को देखा।

TEXT 56

तं निहत्य महाबाहुर्ददाह स्वर्गतश्च सः ।

स चास्य कथयामास शबरीं धर्मचारिणीम् ॥ ५६ ॥

श्रमणीं धर्मनिपुणामभिगच्छेति राघव ।

taṁ nihatya mahā-bāhur dadāha svar-gataś ca saḥ |

sa cāsya kathayām āsa śabarīṁ dharma-cāriṇīm || 56 ||

śramaṇīṁ dharma-nipuṇām abhigaccheti rāghava |

tam– (3rd p. pron. m. acc. sg.) him; **nihatya**– (abs., ni + √ han) having killed; **mahat**– (adj.) long; **bāhu**– (m. n.) arm; **mahā-bāhuḥ**– (bv. cp./m. adj. nom. sg.) he whose arms are long; **dadāha**– (√ dah, perf. 3rd p. sg.) burnt; **svaḥ**– (m. n.) heaven; **gata**– (ppp.) gone; **svar-gataḥ**– (tp. cp. m. nom. sg.) gone to heaven; **ca**– (ind.) and; **saḥ**– (3rd p. pron. m. nom. sg.) He; **saḥ**– (3rd p. pron. m. nom. sg.) he; **ca**– (ind.) and; **asya**– (d. pron. m. gen. sg.) to Him; **kathayām āsa**– (√ kath, perf. 3rd p. sg.) told; **śabarīm**– (f. n. acc. sg.) the ascetic Śabarī; **dharma**– (m. n.) religious observances; **cārin**– (adj.) practicing; **dharma-cāriṇīm**– (tp. cp./f. adj. acc. sg.) practicing religious observances; **śramaṇīm**– (f. n. acc. sg.) ascetic; **dharma**– (m. n.) religious principles; **nipuṇa**– (adj.) expert; **dharma-nipuṇām**– (tp. cp./f. adj. acc. sg.) expert in religious principles; **abhigaccha**– (abhi + √ gam, ipt. 2nd p. sg.) approach; **iti**– (ind.) thus; **rāghava**– (m. n. voc. sg.) O Rāma, descendant of King Raghu.

Prose order

saḥ mahā-bāhuḥ taṁ nihatya dadāha | svar-gataḥ ca saḥ asya kathayām āsa ca "rāghava, dharma-cāriṇīṁ śramaṇīṁ dharma-nipuṇāṁ śabarīm abhigaccha" iti |

Translation

The long-armed Śrī Rāma killed and burnt that rākṣasa, who ascended to heaven while speaking these words: "O Rāghava, you should approach the ascetic Śabarī, who is always performing religious observances and is expert in dharma."

महाबाहु श्री राम ने उस राक्षस का वध करके उसको जला दिया। तब वह स्वर्ग चला गया और बोला "हे राघव, आप धर्मचारिणी धर्म निपुण तपस्विनी शबरी के पास जाइए"।

TEXTS 57 - 58

सोऽभ्यगच्छन् महातेजाः शबरीं शत्रुसूदनः ॥ ५७ ॥

शबर्या पूजितः सम्यग्रामो दशरथात्मजः ।

पम्पातीरे हनुमता संगतो वानरेण ह ॥ ५८ ॥

so'bhyagacchan mahā-tejāḥ śabarīṁ śatru-sūdanaḥ || 57 ||

śabaryā pūjitaḥ samyag rāmo daśarathātmajaḥ |

pampā-tīre hanumatā saṁgato vānareṇa ha || 58 ||

saḥ– (3rd p. pron. m. nom. sg.) He; **abhyagacchat**– (abhi + √ gam, imp. 3rd p. sg.) went; **mahat**– (adj.) great; **tejas**– (neu. n.) power; **mahā-tejāḥ**– (bv. cp./m. adj. nom. sg.) he whose power is great; **śabarīm**– (f. n. acc. sg.) to Śabarī; **śatru**– (m. n.) enemy; **sūdana**– (m. n.) destruction; **śatru-sūdanaḥ**– (tp. cp. m. nom. sg.) he who is the destruction of the enemies; **śabaryā**– (f. n. inst. sg.) by

Śabarī; **pūjitaḥ**– (ppp. m. nom. sg.) worshipped; **samyak**– (ind.) properly; **rāmaḥ**– (m. n. nom. sg.) Śrī Rāma; **daśaratha**– (m. n.) King Daśaratha; **ātman**– (m. n.) self; **ja**– (adj.) born; **daśarathātmajaḥ**– (tp. cp. m. nom. sg.) the son of King Daśaratha; **pampā**– (f. n.) the river Pampā; **tīra**– (neu. n.) bank; **pampā-tīre**– (tp. cp. neu. loc. sg.) on the bank of the river Pampā; **hanumatā**– (m. n. inst. sg.) with Hanumān; **saṁgataḥ**– (ppp. m. nom. sg.) met; **vānareṇa**– (m. n. inst. sg.) with the monkey; **ha**– (ind.) indeed.

Prose order

mahā-tejāḥ śatru-sūdanaḥ saḥ śabarīm abhyagacchat | śabaryā samyak pūjitaḥ daśarathātmajaḥ rāmaḥ pampā-tīre vānareṇa hanumatā saṁgataḥ ha |

Translation

Rāma of great power, the destroyer of enemies, then went to Śabarī's hermitage. Having been properly worshipped by Śabarī, the son of King Daśaratha met the monkey Hanumān[29] *on the bank of the river Pampā.*

तब महातेजस्वी शत्रु सूदन राम शबरी के पास गए। शबरी से अच्छी तरह पूजित होकर, श्री राम पंपा नदी के किनारे पर वानर हनुमान से मिले।

---

[29] The son of the wind-god.

Kiṣkindhā-kāṇḍa

TEXT 59

हनुमद्वचनाच्चैव सुग्रीवेण समागतः ।

सुग्रीवाय च तत् सर्वं शंसद्रामो महाबलः ॥ ५९ ॥

आदितस्तद्यथावृत्तं सीतायाश्च विशेषतः ।

hanumad-vacanāc caiva sugrīveṇa samāgataḥ |

sugrīvāya ca tat sarvaṁ śaṁsad rāmo mahā-balaḥ || 59 ||

āditas tad yathā-vṛttaṁ sītāyāś ca viśeṣataḥ |

hanumat– (m. n.) Hanumān; **vacana**– (neu. n.) words; **hanumad-vacanāt**– (tp. cp. neu. abl. sg.) following Hanumān's advice; **ca**– (ind.) and; **eva**– (ind.) indeed; **sugrīveṇa**– (m. n. inst. sg.) with Sugrīva; **samāgataḥ**– (ppp. m. nom. sg.) met; **sugrīvāya**– (m. n. dat. sg.) to Sugrīva; **ca**– (ind.) and; **tat**– (d. pron. neu. acc. sg.) that; **sarvam**– (adj. pron. neu. acc. sg.) all; **śaṁsat**[30]– (√ śaṁs, imp. 3rd p. sg.) told; **rāmaḥ**– (m. n. nom. sg.) Śrī Rāma; **mahat**– (adj.) great; **bala**– (neu. n.) strength; **mahā-balaḥ**– (bv. cp./m. adj. nom. sg.) he whose strength is great; **ādi-taḥ**– (m. n. + ind.

---

30 The expected verbal form here is *aśaṁsat.* The elision of the affix characteristic of the imperfect tense here is *ārṣa-prayoga,* a kind of poetic licence.

aff.) from the beginning; **tat**– (d. pron. neu. acc. sg.) that; **yathā**– (ind.) as; **vṛtta**– (neu. n.) happening; **yathā-vṛttam**– (ind. cp.) as it happened; **sītāyāḥ**– (f. n. gen. sg.) of Sītā; **ca**– (ind.) and; **viśeṣataḥ**– (m. n. + ind. aff.) especially.

Prose order

hanumad-vacanāt ca eva mahā-balaḥ rāmaḥ sugrīveṇa samāgataḥ sugrīvāya ca āditaḥ tat sarvaṁ sītāyāḥ ca tat viśeṣataḥ yathā-vṛttaṁ śaṁsat|

Translation

Following Hanumān's advice, the powerful Rāma met Sugrīva and told him all that happened from the beginning, especially about Sītā.

हनुमान के वचन से अतिबलवान श्री राम ने सुग्रीव से मिलकर उसको प्रारम्भ से सम्पूर्ण वृत्तांत बताया, विशेष रूप से सीता के बारे में।

TEXT 60

सुग्रीवश्चापि तत् सर्वं श्रुत्वा रामस्य वानरः ॥ ६० ॥

चकार सख्यं रामेण प्रीतश्चैवाग्निसाक्षिकम् ।

sugrīvaś cāpi tat sarvaṁ śrutvā rāmasya vānaraḥ || 60 ||

cakāra sakhyaṁ rāmeṇa prītaś caivāgni-sākṣikam |

sugrīvaḥ– (m. n. nom. sg.) Sugrīva; **ca**– (ind.) and; **api**– (ind.) also; **tat**– (d. pron. neu. acc. sg.) that; **sarvam**– (adj. pron. neu. acc. sg.) all; **śrutvā**– (abs., √śru) having heard; **rāmasya**– (m. n. gen. sg.) Śrī Rāma's; **vānaraḥ**– (m. n. nom. sg.) monkey; **cakāra**– (√ kṛ, perf. 3rd p. sg.) made; **sakhyam**– (neu. n. acc. sg.) friendship; **rāmeṇa**– (m. n. inst. sg.) with Śrī Rāma; **prītaḥ**– (m. adj. nom. sg.) pleased; **ca**– (ind.) and; **eva**– (ind.) indeed; **agni**– (m. n.) fire; **sākṣin**– (m. n.) a witness; **agni-sākṣikam**– (bv. cp./m. adj. acc. sg.) having fire for a witness.

Prose order

vānaraḥ sugrīvaḥ ca api rāmasya tat sarvaṁ śrutvā prītaḥ ca eva rāmeṇa agni-sākṣikaṁ sakhyaṁ cakāra |

Translation

Having heard all that happened to Śrī Rāma, the monkey Sugrīva was pleased to become friends with Him having fire for a witness.

श्री राम का सम्पूर्ण वृत्तांत सुनकर वानर सुग्रीव ने प्रसन्न होते हुए अग्नि को साक्षी मानकर श्री राम के साथ मित्रता की।

TEXT 61

ततो वानरराजेन वैरानुकथनं प्रति ॥ ६१ ॥

रामायावेदितं सर्वं प्रणयाद् दुःखितेन च ।

tato vānara-rājena vairānukathanaṁ prati || 61 ||

rāmāyāveditaṁ sarvaṁ praṇayād duḥkhitena ca |

tataḥ– (ind.) after that; **vānara**– (m. n.) monkey; **rājan**– (m. n.) king; **vānara-rājena**– (tp. cp. m. inst. sg.) by the King of the monkeys; **vaira**– (neu. n.) enmity; **anukathanam**– (neu. n.) discussion; **vairānukathanam**– (tp. cp. neu. acc. sg.) the discussion about the enmity with Vāli; **prati**– (ind.) concerning; **rāmāyā**– (m. n. dat. sg.) to Śrī Rāma; **āveditam**– (ppp. neu. acc. sg.) told; **sarvam**– (adj. pron. neu. acc. sg.) everything; **praṇayāt**– (m. n. abl. sg.) confidentially; **duḥkhitena**– (m. adj. inst. sg.) distressed; **ca**– (ind.) also.

Prose order

tataḥ duḥkhitena vānara-rājena ca rāmāya sarvam vairānukathanaṁ prati praṇayāt āveditam |

Translation

After that, the distressed King of the monkeys, Sugrīva, also confidentially told Śrī Rāma everything about his enmity toward Vāli.

तत्पश्चात् दुःखित वानरराज ने भी विश्वास करके श्री राम को वालि से अपनी शत्रुता के बारे में सब कुछ सुनाया।

TEXTS 62 - 63

प्रतिज्ञातं च रामेण तदा वालिवधं प्रति ॥ ६२ ॥

वालिनश्च बलं तत्र कथयामास वानरः ।

सुग्रीवः शङ्कितश्चासीन्नित्यं वीर्येण राघवे ॥ ६३ ॥

pratijñātaṁ ca rāmeṇa tadā vāli-vadhaṁ prati || 62 ||

vālinaś ca balaṁ tatra kathayām āsa vānaraḥ |

sugrīvaḥ śaṅkitaś cāsīn nityaṁ vīryeṇa rāghave || 63 ||

pratijñātam– (ppp. m. acc. sg.) promised; **ca**– (ind.) and; **rāmeṇa**– (m. n. inst. sg.) by Śrī Rāma; **tadā**– (ind) then; **vāli**– (m. n.) Vāli; **vadha**– (m. n.) killing; **vāli-vadham**– (tp. cp./m. n. acc. sg.) the killing of Vāli; **prati**– (ind.) concerning; **vālinaḥ**– (m. n. gen. sg.) of Vāli; **ca**– (ind.) and; **balam**– (neu. n. acc. sg.) strength; **tatra**– (ind.) then; **kathayām āsa**– (√ kath, perf. 3rd p. sg.) told; **vānaraḥ**– (m. n. nom. sg.) monkey; **sugrīvaḥ**– (m. n. nom. sg.) Sugrīva; **śaṅkitaḥ**– (ppp. m. nom. sg.) doubtful; **ca**– (ind.) however; **āsīt**– (√ as, imp. 3rd p. sg.) was; **nityam**– (ind.) constantly; **vīryeṇa**– (neu. n. inst. sg.) by strength; **rāghave**– (m. n. loc. sg.) in Śrī Rāma.

Prose order

tadā ca rāmeṇa vāli-vadhaṁ prati pratijñātam | vānaraḥ sugrīvaḥ ca rāghave vīryeṇa nityaṁ śaṅkitaḥ āsīt tatra ca vālinaḥ balaṁ kathayām āsa |

Translation

Then Śrī Rāma promised to kill Vāli. However, the monkey Sugrīva constantly doubted Rāma's strength, and therefore he told Him of Vāli's strength.

तब श्री राम ने वालि के वध की प्रतिज्ञा की। सुग्रीव को श्री राम की वीरता पर हमेशा संदिग्धता थी, इसलिये उसने राम को वालि के बल का वर्णन सुनाया।

TEXT 64

राघवप्रत्ययार्थं तु दुन्दुभेः कायमुत्तमम् ।

दर्शयामास सुग्रीवो महापर्वतसन्निभम् ॥ ६४ ॥

rāghava-pratyayārthaṁ tu dundubheḥ kāyam uttamam |

darśayām āsa sugrīvo mahā-parvata-sannibham || 64 ||

rāghava– (m. n.) Śrī Rāma; **pratyaya**– (m. n.) conviction; **artha**– (m. n.) purpose; **rāghava-pratyayārtham**– (tp. cp./ind.) in order to convince Śrī Rāma; **tu**– (ind.) then; **dundubheḥ**– (m. n. gen. sg.) of Dundubhi[31]; **kāyam**– (m. n. acc. sg.) body; **uttamam**– (m.

[31] This was a demon killed by Vāli.

adj. acc. sg.) very high; **darśayām āsa**– (darśay[32], perf. 3rd p. sg.) showed; **sugrīvaḥ**– (m. n. nom. sg.) sugrīva; **mahat**– (adj.) huge; **parvata**– (m. n.) mountain; **sannibha**– (adj.) similar; **mahā-parvata-sannibham**– (tp. cp./m. adj. acc. sg.) similar to a huge mountain.

Prose order

sugrīvaḥ tu rāghava-pratyayārthaṁ dundubheḥ uttamaṁ mahā-parvata-sannibhaṁ kāyaṁ darśayām āsa |

Translation

In order to convince Śrī Rāma of Vāli's power, he showed Him the dead body of Dundubhi, which was huge and high like a mountain.

वालि के बल के बारे में श्री राम को आश्वस्त करने के लिये सुग्रीव ने उनको दुंदुभि का शरीर दिखवाया, जो ऊँचा और महान पर्वत के समान था।

TEXT 65

उत्स्मयित्वा महाबाहुः प्रेक्ष्य चास्थि महाबलः ।

पादाङ्गुष्ठेन चिक्षेप सम्पूर्णं दशयोजनम् ॥ ६५ ॥

utsmayitvā mahā-bāhuḥ prekṣya cāsthi mahā-balaḥ |

---

[32] This is the causative verbal form of the root *dṛś.*

pādāṅguṣṭhena cikṣepa sampūrṇaṁ daśa-yojanam || 65 ||

utsmayitvā– (abs., ut + √ smi) having smiled; **mahat**– (adj.) long; **bāhu**– (m. n.) arm; **mahā-bāhuḥ**– (bv. cp./m. adj. nom. sg.) he whose arms are long; **prekṣya**– (abs., pra + √ īkṣ) having looked at; **ca**– (ind.) and; **asthi**– (neu. n. acc. sg.) bone; **mahat**– (adj.) great; **bala**– (neu. n.) strength; **mahā-balaḥ**– (bv. cp./m. adj. nom. sg.) he whose strength is great; **pāda**– (m. n.) foot; **aṅguṣṭha**– (m. n.) toe; **pādāṅguṣṭhena**– (tp. cp. m. inst. sg.) with the toe; **cikṣepa**– (√ kṣip, perf. 3rd p. sg.) threw; **sampūrṇam**– (adj. neu. acc. sg.) whole; **daśa**– (num.) ten; **yojana**– (neu. n.) a distance of nine miles; **daśa-yojanam**– (tp. cp. neu. acc. sg.) ninety miles.

Prose order

mahā-bāhuḥ mahā-balaḥ ca asthi prekṣya utsmayitvā pādāṅguṣṭhena sampūrṇaṁ daśa-yojanaṁ cikṣepa |

Translation

The long-armed Rāma, being very powerful, smiled after looking at Dundubhi's bones, and kicking with His toe, He threw all of them ninety miles away.

महाबाहु अतिबलवान राम ने दुंदुभि की हड्डी देखकर मुस्कराते हुए अपने पैर के अंगूठे से उसको दस योजन दूर फेंका।

TEXT 66

बिभेद च पुनस्तालान् सप्तैकेन महेषुणा ।

गिरिं रसातलं चैव जनयन् प्रत्ययं तदा ॥ ६६ ॥

bibheda ca punas tālān saptaikena maheṣuṇā |

giriṁ rasātalaṁ caiva janayan pratyayaṁ tadā || 66 ||

bibheda– (√ bhid, perf. 3rd p. sg.) pierced; **ca**– (ind.) and; **punaḥ**– (ind.) further; **tālān**– (m. n. acc. pl.) palmyra trees; **sapta**– (num. acc. pl.) seven; **ekena**– (num. m. inst. sg.) with one; **mahat**– (adj.) big; **iṣu**– (m. n.) arrow; **maheṣuṇā**– (tp. cp. m. inst. sg.) with a big arrow; **girim**– (m. n. acc. sg.) mountain; **rasātalam**– (neu. n. acc. sg.) Rasātala[33]; **ca**– (ind.) and; **eva**– (ind.) indeed; **janayan**– (janay[34], m. prp. 3rd p. nom. sg.) producing; **pratyayam**– (m. n. acc. sg.) conviction; **tadā**– (ind.) then.

Prose order

tadā punaḥ ca pratyayaṁ janayan ekena maheṣuṇā sapta tālān giriṁ rasātalaṁ ca eva bibheda |

Translation

[33] The seventh region in the nether world.

[34] This is the causative verbal form of the root *jan*.

Then, further increasing Sugrīva's conviction, with a single large arrow Śrī Rāma pierced seven Palmyra trees, one mountain and Rasātala.

तब फिर सुग्रीव का विश्वास उत्पन्न करते हुए एक ही महान बाण से श्री राम ने सात ताल वृक्षों, एक पर्वत और रसातल को छेद किया।

TEXT 67

ततः प्रीतमनास्तेन विश्वस्तः स महाकपिः ।

किष्किन्धां रामसहितो जगाम च गुहां तदा ॥ ६७ ॥

tataḥ prīta-manās tena viśvastaḥ sa mahā-kapiḥ |

kiṣkindhāṁ rāma-sahito jagāma ca guhāṁ tadā || 67 ||

tataḥ– (ind.) after that; **prīta**– (adj.) pleased; **manas**– (neu. n.) mind; **prīta-manāḥ**– (bv. cp./m. adj. nom. sg.) he whose mind is pleased; **tena**– (d. pron. neu. inst. sg.) by that; **viśvastaḥ**– (ppp. m. nom. sg.) convinced; **saḥ**– (d. pron. m. nom. sg.) that; **mahat**– (adj.) great; **kapi**– (m. n.) monkey; **mahā-kapiḥ**– (tp. cp. m. nom. sg.) great monkey; **kiṣkindhām**– (f. n. acc. sg.) named Kiṣkindhā; **rāma**– (m. n.) Śrī Rāma; **sahita**– (adj.) together with; **rāma-sahitaḥ**– (tp. cp./m. adj. nom. sg.) accompanied by Rāma; **jagāma**– (√ gam, perf. 3rd p. sg.) went; **ca**– (ind.) and; **guhām**– (f. n. acc. sg.) cave; **tadā**– (ind.) then.

Prose order

tataḥ saḥ mahā-kapiḥ tena viśvastaḥ prīta-manāḥ ca (bhūtvā) tadā rāma-sahitaḥ kiṣkindhāṁ guhāṁ jagāma |

Translation

Being convinced by those feats, with a pleased mind, that great monkey went to the Kiṣkindhā cave accompanied by Śrī Rāma.

उस अतिमानवीय कार्य से विश्वस्त होकर प्रसन्न मन से वह महान कपि श्री राम के साथ किष्किंधा गुफा चला गया।

TEXT 68

ततोऽगर्जद्धरिवरः सुग्रीवो हेमपिङ्गलः ।

तेन नादेन महता निर्जगाम हरीश्वरः ॥ ६८ ॥

tato'garjad dhari-varaḥ sugrīvo hema-piṅgalaḥ |

tena nādena mahatā nirjagāma harīśvaraḥ || 68 ||

tataḥ– (ind.) then; **agarjat**– (√ garj, imp. 3rd p. sg.) roared; **hari**– (m. n.) monkey; **vara**– (adj.) best; **hari-varaḥ**– (tp. cp./m. adj. nom. sg.) the best of monkeys; **sugrīvaḥ**– (m. n. nom. sg.) Sugrīva; **heman**– (neu. n.) gold; **piṅgala**– (adj.) yellow; **hema-piṅgalaḥ**– (tp. cp./m. adj. nom. sg.) yellow like gold; **tena**– (d. pron. m. inst. sg.) because of that; **nādena**– (m. n. inst. sg.) by the sound; **mahatā**– (m. adj. inst. sg.) big; **nirjagāma**– (nir + √ gam, perf. 3rd p. sg.) came out; **hari**– (m. n.) monkey; **īśvara**– (m. n.) king; **harīśvaraḥ**– (tp. cp. m. nom. sg.) the King of the monkeys.

Prose order

tataḥ hema-piṅgalaḥ hari-varaḥ sugrīvaḥ agarjat | harīśvaraḥ tena mahatā nādena nirjagāma |

Translation

The best of monkeys, Sugrīva, whose hue is yellow like gold, then yelled out loudly. Due to that loud noise, the King of the monkeys, Vāli, came out.

तब सुवर्ण के सदृश पीत रंग वाले कपिश्रेष्ठ सुग्रीव ने गर्जना की। उस महान नाद के कारण कपिराज वालि बाहर निकला।

TEXT 69

अनुमान्य तदा तारां सुग्रीवेण समागतः ।

निजघान च तत्रैनं शरेणैकेन राघवः ॥ ६९ ॥

anumānya tadā tārāṁ sugrīveṇa samāgataḥ |

nijaghāna ca tatrainaṁ śareṇaikena rāghavaḥ || 69 ||

anumānya– (abs., anu + mānay[35]) having taking permission; **tadā**– (ind.) at that moment; **tārām**– (f. n. acc. sg.) his wife Tārā; **sugrīveṇa**– (m. n. inst. sg.) with Sugrīva; **samāgataḥ**– (ppp. m. nom. sg.) met; **nijaghāna**– (ni + √ han, per. 3rd p. sg.) killed; **ca**– (ind.) and; **tatra**– (ind.) there; **enam**– (d. pron. m. acc. sg.) him; **śareṇa**– (m. n. inst. sg.) arrow; **ekena**– (num. m. inst. sg.) with one; **rāghavaḥ**– (m. n. nom. sg.) Śrī Rāma.

Prose order

tadā tārām anumānya sugrīveṇa samāgataḥ | rāghavaḥ ca ekena śareṇa tatra enaṁ nijaghāna |

Translation

At that moment, having asked permission from his wife Tārā, Vāli met Sugrīva for a duel, and Śrī Rāma killed him on the spot with a single arrow.

उस समय अपनी पत्नी तारा से अनुमति लेकर वालि युद्ध के लिये सुग्रीव से मिला तथा श्री राम ने एक ही बाण से वहीं पर उसका वध किया।

TEXT 70

ततः सुग्रीववचनाद्धत्वा वालिनमाहवे ।

सुग्रीवमेव तद्राज्ये राघवः प्रत्यपादयत् ॥ ७० ॥

---

35 This is the causative verbal form of the root *man*.

tataḥ sugrīva-vacanād dhatvā vālinam āhave |

sugrīvam eva tad-rājye rāghavaḥ pratyapādayat || 70 ||

tataḥ– (ind.) after that; **sugrīva**– (m. n.) Sugrīva; **vacana**– (neu. n.) words; **sugrīva-vacanāt**– (tp. cp. neu. abl. sg.) due to Sugrīva's words; **hatvā**– (abs., √ han) having killed; **vālinam**– (m. n. acc. sg.) Vāli; **āhave**– (m. n. loc. sg.) in the battle; **sugrīvam**– (m. n. acc. sg.) Sugrīva; **eva**– (ind.) indeed; **tat**– (d. pron.) of his; **rājya**– (neu. n.) kingdom; **tad-rājye**– (tp. cp. neu. loc. sg.) in his kingdom; **rāghavaḥ**– (m. n. nom. sg.) Śrī Rāma; **pratyapādayat**– (prati + pāday[36], imp. 3rd p. sg.) established.

Prose order

rāghavaḥ sugrīva-vacanāt āhave vālinaṁ hatvā tataḥ tad-rājye sugrīvam eva pratyapādayat |

Translation

Having killed Vāli in the battle at the request of Sugrīva, Śrī Rāma set Sugrīva on the throne of Vāli's kingdom.

सुग्रीव के कहने पर युद्ध में वालि का वध करके श्री राम ने उसके बाद सुग्रीव को ही वालि के राज्य में स्थापित किया।

TEXT 71

---

[36] This is the causative verbal form of the root *pad.*

स च सर्वान् समानीय वानरान् वानरर्षभः ।

दिशः प्रस्थापयामास दिदृक्षुर्जनकात्मजाम् ॥ ७१ ॥

sa ca sarvān samānīya vānarān vānararṣabhaḥ |

diśaḥ prasthāpayām āsa didṛkṣur janakātmajām || 71 ||

saḥ– (3rd p. pron. m. nom. sg.) he; **ca**– (ind.) and; **sarvān**– (adj. pron. m. acc. pl.) all; **samānīya**– (abs., sam + ā + √nī) having assembled; **vānarān**– (m. n. acc. pl.) monkeys; **vānara**– (m.n.) monkey; **ṛṣabha**– (adj.) best; **vānararṣabhaḥ**– (tp. cp./m. adj. nom. sg.) the best of monkeys; **diśaḥ**– (f. n. acc. pl.) directions; **prasthāpayām āsa**– (pra + sthāpay[37], perf. 3rd p. sg.) sent out; **didṛkṣuḥ**– (m. adj. nom. sg.) desiring to find; **janaka**– (m. n.) King Janaka; **ātman**– (neu. n.) self; **ja**– (adj.) born; **janakātmajām**– (tp. cp./f. adj. acc. sg.) King Janaka's daughter.

Prose order

saḥ ca vānararṣabhaḥ janakātmajāṁ didṛkṣuḥ sarvān vānarān samānīya diśaḥ prasthāpayām āsa |

Translation

With a desire to find Sītā, Sugrīva, best among monkeys, gathered all the monkeys and sent them out in all directions.

[37] This is the causative verbal form of the root *sthā*.

सीता का पता लगाने के इच्छुक उस कपिश्रेष्ठ ने सब वानरों को एकत्र करके उनको चारों दिशाओं में भेजा।

Sundara-kāṇḍa

TEXT 72

ततो गृध्रस्य वचनात् सम्पातेर्हनुमान् बली ।
शतयोजनविस्तीर्णं पुप्लुवे लवणार्णवम् ॥ ७२ ॥

tato gṛdhrasya vacanāt sampāter hanumān balī |

śata-yojana-vistīrṇaṁ pupluve lavaṇārṇavam || 72 ||

tataḥ– (ind.) afterwards; **gṛdhrasya**– (m. n. gen. sg.) of the vulture; **vacanāt**– (neu. n. abl. sg.) on account of the words; **sampāteḥ**– (m. n. gen. sg.) of Sampāti; **hanumān**– (m. n. nom. sg.) Hanumān; **balī**– (m. adj. nom. sg.) powerful; **śata**– (num.) one hundred; **yojana**– (neu. n.) nine miles; **vistīrṇa**– (ppp./adj.) extended; **śata-yojana-vistīrṇam**– (tp. cp./m. adj. acc. sg.) extended through nine hundred miles; **pupluve**– (√plu, perf. 3rd p. sg.) jumped; **lavaṇa**–(neu. n.) salt water; **arṇava**– (m. n.) ocean; **lavaṇārṇavam**– (tp. cp./m. n. acc. sg.) the ocean of salt water.

Prose order

tataḥ balī hanumān sampāteḥ gṛdhrasya vacanāt śata-yojana-vistīrṇaṁ lavaṇārṇavaṁ pupluve |

Translation

Then, following the instructions of the vulture Sampāti,[38] *Hanumān jumped over the ocean, which extended a distance of nine hundred miles.*

उसके बाद सम्पाति नामक गिद्ध के वचन के अनुसार बलवान हनुमान एक सौ योजन विस्तीर्ण क्षार समुद्र लाँघ गये।

TEXT 73

तत्र लङ्कां समासाद्य पुरीं रावणपालिताम् ।

ददर्श सीतां ध्यायन्तीमशोकवनिकां गताम् ॥ ७३ ॥

tatra laṅkāṁ samāsādya purīṁ rāvaṇa-pālitām |

dadarśa sītāṁ dhyāyantīm aśoka-vanikāṁ gatām || 73 ||

tatra– (ind.) there; **laṅkām**– (f. n. acc. sg.) Laṅkā; **samāsādya**– (abs., sam + ā + sāday[39]) having reached; **purīm**– (f. n. acc. sg.) city; **rāvaṇa**– (m. n.) Rāvaṇa; **pālita**– (ppp./adj.) protected; **rāvaṇa-pālitām**– (tp. cp./f. adj. acc. sg.) protected by Rāvaṇa;

---

[38] Jaṭāyu's elder brother.

[39] This is the causative verbal form of the root *sad.*

dadarśa– (√ dṛś, perf. 3rd p. sg.) saw; **sītām**– (f. n. acc. sg.) Sītā; **dhyāyantīm**– (√ dhyai, f. prp. acc. sg.) pensive; **aśoka**– (m. n.) Aśoka tree; **vanikā**– (f. n.) grove; **aśoka-vanikām**– (tp. cp. f. acc. sg.) the Aśoka grove; **gatām**– (ppp. f. acc. sg.) situated in.

Prose order

tatra rāvaṇa-pālitāṁ laṅkāṁ purīṁ samāsādya aśoka-vanikāṁ gatāṁ dhyāyantīṁ sītāṁ dadarśa |

Translation

Having reached the city of Laṅkā, which was protected by Rāvaṇa, Hanumān saw the pensive Sītā in the Aśoka grove.

रावण के द्वारा सुरक्षित लंका पुरी पहुँच कर हनुमान ने अशोक वाटिका में स्थित चिंतामग्न सीता को देखा।

TEXT 74

निवेदयित्वाभिज्ञानं प्रवृत्तिं च निवेद्य च ।

समाश्वास्य च वैदेहीं मर्दयामास तोरणम् ॥ ७४ ॥

nivedayitvābhijñānaṁ pravṛttiṁ ca nivedya ca |

samāśvāsya ca vaidehīṁ mardayām āsa toraṇam || 74 ||

nivedayitvā– (abs., ni + veday[40]) having presented; **abhijñānam**– (neu. n. acc. sg.) token; **pravṛttim**– (f. n. acc. sg.) news; **ca**– (ind.) and; **nivedya**– (abs., ni + √ vid) having informed; **ca**– (ind.) and; **samāśvāsya**– (abs., sam + ā + śvāsay[41]) having cheered up; **ca**– (ind.) and; **vaidehīm**– (f. n. acc. sg.) to Sītā, the daughter of the King of Videha; **mardayām āsa**– (marday[42], perf. 3rd p. sg.) crushed; **toraṇam**– (neu. n. acc. sg.) gate.

Prose order

abhijñānaṁ ca nivedayitvā pravṛttiṁ ca nivedya vaidehīṁ ca samāśvāsya toraṇaṁ mardayām āsa |

Translation

Having presented the token given to him by Śrī Rāma and informed Sītā about the news, Hanumān cheered her up. He then crushed the gate of the grove.

श्री राम की निशानी देकर और समाचार सुनाकर हनुमान ने सीता को आश्वासन दिया। उसके बाद उन्होंने उस वाटिका का द्वार खंडित किया।

TEXT 75

पञ्च सेनाग्रगान् हत्वा सप्त मन्त्रिसुतानपि ।

---

[40] This is the causative verbal form of the root *vid.*

[41] This is the causative verbal form of the root *śvas*

[42] This is the causative verbal form of the root *mṛd.*

शूरमक्षं च निष्पिष्य ग्रहणं समुपागमत् ॥ ७५ ॥

pañca senāgragān hatvā sapta mantri-sutān api |

śūram akṣaṁ ca niṣpiṣya grahaṇaṁ samupāgamat || 75 ||

pañca– (num. acc. pl.) five; **senā**– (f. n.) army; **agra**– (neu. n.) front; **ga**– (adj.) going; **senāgragān**– (tp. cp. m. acc. pl.) leaders of the army; **hatvā**– (abs., √han) having killed; **sapta**– (num. acc. pl.) seven; **mantri**– (m. n.) minister; **suta**– (m. n.) son; **mantri-sutān**– (tp. cp. m. acc. sg.) sons of the ministers; **api**– (ind.) also; **śūram**– (m. adj. acc. sg.) heroic; **akṣam**– (m. n. acc. sg.) Akṣa, Rāvaṇa's son; **ca**– (ind.) and; **niṣpiṣya**– (abs., niṣ + √piṣ) having crushed; **grahaṇam**– (neu. n. acc. sg.) captivity; **samupāgamat**– (sam + upa + √ gam, imp. 3rd p. sg.) went into.

Prose order

pañca senāgragān sapta mantri-sutān api hatvā śūram akṣaṁ ca niṣpiṣya grahaṇaṁ samupāgamat |

Translation

After killing five leaders of the army, seven sons of the ministers and crushing the heroic Akṣa, Hanumān let himself to be captured.

पाँच सेनापतियों, सात मंत्री पुत्रों तथा वीर अक्ष को मारने के बाद हनुमान जानबूझकर बंदी हो गये।

TEXT 76

अस्त्रेणोन्मुक्तमात्मानं ज्ञात्वा पैतामहाद्वरात् ।

मर्षयन् राक्षसान् वीरो यन्त्रिणस्तान् यदृच्छया ॥ ७६ ॥

astreṇonmuktam ātmānaṁ jñātvā paitāmahād varāt |

marṣayan rākṣasān vīro yantriṇas tān yadṛcchayā || 76 ||

astreṇa– (neu. n. inst. sg.) by the weapon; **unmuktam**– (ppp./neu. adj. acc. sg.) free from; **ātmānam**– (m. n. acc. sg./ind.) oneself; **jñātvā**– (abs., √jñā) having known; **paitāmahāt**– (m. adj. abl. sg.) related to grandfather Brahmā; **varāt**– (m. n. abl. sg.) because of a benediction; **marṣayan**– (marṣay[43], m. prp. nom. sg.) patiently bearing; **rākṣasān**– (m. n. acc. pl.) the demons; **vīraḥ**– (m. n. nom. sg.) the hero; **yantriṇaḥ**– (m. adj. acc. pl.) harassers; **tān**– (d. pron. m. acc. pl.) them; **yadṛcchayā**– (ind.) voluntarily.

Prose order

paitāmahāt varāt astreṇa unmuktam ātmānaṁ jñātvā tān yantriṇaḥ rākṣasān yadṛcchayā marṣayan vīraḥ |

Translation

Knowing that he could free himself from any weapon because of a benediction given to him by Lord Brahmā, the heroic

[43] This is the causative verbal form of the root *mṛṣ*.

Hanumān voluntarily tolerated the rākṣasas who were harassing him.

ब्रह्मा के वरदान से अपने को अस्त्रों से मुक्त जानकर वीर हनुमान ने अपनी इच्छा से सताने वाले राक्षसों को सह लिया।

TEXT 77

ततो दग्ध्वा पुरीं लङ्कामृते सीतां च मैथिलीम् ।

रामाय प्रियमाख्यातुं पुनरायान् महाकपिः ॥ ७७ ॥

tato dagdhvā purīṁ laṅkām ṛte sītāṁ ca maithilīm |

rāmāya priyam ākhyātuṁ punar āyān mahā-kapiḥ || 77 ||

tataḥ– (ind.) then; **dagdhvā**– (abs., √ dah) having burnt; **purīm**– (f. n. acc. sg.) the city; **laṅkām**– (f. n. acc. sg.) Laṅkā; **ṛte**– (ind.) except for; **sītām**– (f. n. acc. sg.) Sītā; **ca**– (ind.) and; **maithilīm**– (f. adj. acc. sg.) the daughter of the King of Mithilā; **rāmāya**– (m. n. dat. sg.) to Śrī rāma; **priyam**– (neu. adj. acc. sg.) the happy news; **ākhyātum**– (ā + √ khyā, inf.) to tell; **punaḥ**– (ind.) again; **āyāt**– (ā + √yā, imp. 3rd p. sg.) went; **mahat**– (adj.) great; **kapi**– (m. n.) monkey; **mahā-kapiḥ**– (tp. cp./m. adj. nom. sg.) great monkey.

Prose order

tataḥ ca mahā-kapiḥ maithilīṁ sītām ṛte laṅkāṁ purīṁ dagdhvā rāmāya priyam ākhyātuṁ punaḥ āyāt |

Translation

Then the great Hanumān burnt the whole city of Laṅkā aside from Sītā's place, and returned to Śrī Rāma to tell the happy news.

तब सीता के स्थान के अतिरिक्त सारी लंका पुरी को जला कर महाकपि हनुमान फिर से शुभ समाचार बताने श्री राम के पास गये।

TEXT 78

सोऽभिगम्य महात्मानं कृत्वा रामं प्रदक्षिणम् ।

न्यवेदयदमेयात्मा दृष्टा सीतेति तत्त्वतः ॥ ७८ ॥

so'bhigamya mahātmānaṁ kṛtvā rāmaṁ pradakṣiṇam |

nyavedayad ameyātmā dṛṣṭā sīteti tattvataḥ || 78 ||

saḥ– (3rd p. pron. m. nom. sg.) he; **abhigamya**– (abs., abhi + √ gam) having approached; **mahat**– (adj.) great; **ātman**– (m. n.) soul; **mahātmānam**– (bv. cp./m. adj. acc. sg.) great soul; **kṛtvā**– (abs., √ kṛ) having done; **rāmam**– (m. n. acc. sg.) Śrī Rāma; **pradakṣiṇam**– (neu. n. acc. sg.) circumambulation; **nyavedayat**–

(ni + veday[44], imp. 3rd p. sg.) informed; **ameya–** (adj.) immeasurable; **ātman–** (m. n.) heart; **ameyātmā–** (bv. cp./m. adj. nom. sg.) he whose heart is immeasurable, magnanimous; **dṛṣṭā–** (ppp. f. nom. sg.) seen; **sītā–** (f. n. nom. sg.) Sītā; **iti–** (ind.) thus; **tattva-taḥ–** (neu. n. + ind. aff.) factually.

Prose order

saḥ ameyātmā mahātmānaṁ rāmam abhigamya pradakṣiṇaṁ kṛtvā "sītā tattvataḥ dṛṣṭā" iti nyavedayat |

Translation

Approaching the great soul Rāma, the magnanimous Hanumān circumambulated Him and informed Him: "I have definitely seen Sītā."

महात्मा श्री राम के पास जाकर उनकी प्रदक्षिणा करके अत्युदार हनुमान ने निवेदन किया कि "मैंने निश्चय सीता जी को देखा"।

Yuddha-kāṇḍa

TEXT 79

ततः सुग्रीवसहितो गत्वा तीरं महोदधेः ।

---

[44] This is the causative verbal form of the root *vid.*

समुद्रं क्षोभयामास शरैरादित्यसन्निभैः ॥ ७९ ॥

tataḥ sugrīva-sahito gatvā tīraṁ mahodadheḥ |

samudraṁ kṣobhayām āsa śarair āditya-sannibhaiḥ || 79 ||

tataḥ– (ind.) after that; **sugrīva**– (m. n.) Sugrīva; **sahita**– (adj.) together with; **sugrīva-sahitaḥ**– (tp. cp./m. adj. nom. sg.) together with Sugrīva; **gatvā**– (abs., √gam) having gone; **tīram**– (neu. n. acc. sg.) shore; **mahat**– (adj.) great; **uda**– (neu. n.) water; **dhi**– (m. n.) receptacle; **mahodadheḥ**– (m. n. gen. sg.) of the great ocean; **samudram**– (m. n. acc. sg.) the ocean; **kṣobhayām āsa**– (kṣobhay[45], perf. 3rd p. sg.) agitated; **śaraiḥ**– (m. n. inst. pl.) with arrows; **āditya**– (m. n.) the sun; **sannibha**– (adj.) similar; **āditya-sannibhaiḥ**– (tp. cp./m. adj. inst. pl.) blazing like the sun.

Prose order

tataḥ sugrīva-sahitaḥ mahodadheḥ tīraṁ gatvā āditya-sannibhaiḥ śaraiḥ samudraṁ kṣobhayām āsa |

Translation

Accompanied by Sugrīva, Śrī Rāma went to the shore of the ocean and agitated it with arrows that blazed like the sun.

तत्पश्चात् सुग्रीव के साथ श्री राम ने महासागर के तट पर जाकर सूर्य के समान बाणों से उसको क्षुब्ध किया।

---

[45] This is the causative verbal form of the root *kṣubh*.

TEXT 80

दर्शयामास चात्मानं समुद्रः सरितां पतिः ।

समुद्रवचनाच्चैव नलं सेतुमकारयत् ॥ ८० ॥

darśayām āsa cātmānaṁ samudraḥ saritāṁ patiḥ |

samudra-vacanāc caiva nalaṁ setum akārayat || 80 ||

darśayām āsa– (darśay[46], perf. 3rd p. sg.) showed; **ca**– (ind.) also; **ātmānam**– (m. n. acc. sg./ind.) himself; **samudraḥ**– (m. n. nom. sg.) the ocean; **saritām**– (f. n. gen. pl.) of streams; **patiḥ**– (m. n. nom. sg.) lord; **samudra**– (m. n.) ocean; **vacana**– (neu. n.) words; **samudra-vacanāt**– (tp. cp. neu. abl. sg.) on accounts of the words of the ocean; **ca**– (ind.) and; **eva**– (ind.) indeed; **nalam**– (m. n. acc. sg.) the monkey called Nala; **setum**– (m. n. acc. sg.) bridge; **akārayat**– (kāray[47], imp. 3rd p. sg.) caused to be done.

Prose order

saritāṁ patiḥ samudraḥ ca ātmānaṁ darśayām āsa | samudra-vacanāt ca eva nalaṁ setum akārayat |

Translation

[46] This is the causative verbal form of the root *dṛś*.

[47] This is the causative verbal form of the root *kṛ*.

The ocean, the lord of all streams, appeared personally, and under his direction, Śrī Rāma had the monkey Nala make a bridge.

नदीपति समुद्र स्वयं प्रकट हो गये और उनके वचन से श्री राम ने नल द्वारा एक पुल बनवाया।

TEXT 81

तेन गत्वा पुरीं लङ्कां हत्वा रावणमाहवे ।
रामः सीतामनुप्राप्य परां व्रीडामुपागमत् ॥ ८१ ॥

tena gatvā purīṁ laṅkāṁ hatvā rāvaṇam āhave |

rāmaḥ sītām anuprāpya parāṁ vrīḍām upāgamat || 81 ||

tena– (d. pron. m. inst. sg.) by that bridge; **gatvā**– (abs., √ gam) having gone; **purīm**– (f. n. acc. sg.) city; **laṅkām**– (f. n. acc. sg.) Laṅkā; **hatvā**– (abs., √ han) having killed; **rāvaṇam**– (m. n. acc. sg.) Rāvaṇa; **āhave**– (m. n. loc. sg.) in the battle; **rāmaḥ**– (m. n. nom. sg.) Śrī Rāma; **sītām**– (f. n. acc. sg.) Sītā; **anuprāpya**– (abs., anu + pra + √ āp) having gotten back; **parām**– (f. adj. acc. sg.) excessive; **vrīḍām**– (f. n. acc. sg.) embarassment; **upāgamat**– (upa + √ gam, aor. 3rd p. sg.) attained.

Prose order

rāmaḥ tena laṅkāṁ purīṁ gatvā āhave rāvaṇam hatvā sītām anuprāpya parāṁ vrīḍām upāgamat |

Translation

After reaching the city of Laṅkā by that bridge, having killed Rāvaṇa in battle and gotten back Sītā, Śrī Rāma then faced great embarrassment.

उस पुल से लंका पुरी जाकर युद्ध में रावण को मारकर सीता जी को पाकर श्री राम बहुत लज्जित हो गये।

TEXT 82

तामुवाच ततो रामः परुषं जनसंसदि ।

अमृष्यमाणा सा सीता विवेश ज्वलनं सती ॥ ८२ ॥

tām uvāca tato rāmaḥ paruṣaṁ jana-saṁsadi |

amṛṣyamāṇā sā sītā viveśa jvalanaṁ satī || 82 ||

tām– (3rd p. pron. f. acc. sg.) to her; **uvāca**– (√ vac, perf. 3rd p. sg.) spoke; **tataḥ**– (ind.) then; **rāmaḥ**– (m. n. nom. sg.) Śrī Rāma; **paruṣam**– (neu. n. acc. sg./ind.) harshly; **jana**– (m. n.) people; **saṁsad**– (f. n.) assembly; **jana-saṁsadi**– (tp. cp. f. loc. sg.) in the assembly of the people; **amṛṣyamāṇā**– (√ mṛṣ, f. pr.pp. nom. sg.)

not tolerating; **sā**– (3rd p. pron. f. nom. sg.) she; **sītā**– (f. n. nom. sg.) Sītā; **viveśa**– (√ viś, perf. 3rd p. sg.) entered; **jvalanam**– (m. n. acc. sg.) fire; **satī**– (f. adj. nom. sg.) chaste.

Prose order

tataḥ jana-saṁsadi rāmaḥ tāṁ paruṣam uvāca | amṛṣyamāṇā sā satī sītā jvalanaṁ viveśa |

Translation

Being unable to tolerate the harsh words that Śrī Rāma spoke in the middle of the assembled people, the chaste Sītā thus entered the fire.

तब श्री राम ने लोगों के समक्ष सीता से कठोर वचन कहे। उन्हें न सहकर सती सीता ने अग्नि में प्रवेश किया।

TEXTS 83 - 84

ततोऽग्निवचनात् सीतां ज्ञात्वा विगतकल्मषाम् ।

कर्मणा तेन महता त्रैलोक्यं सचराचरम् ॥ ८३ ॥

सदेवर्षिगणं तुष्टं राघवस्य महात्मनः ।

बभौ रामः सम्प्रहृष्टः पूजितः सर्वदैवतैः ॥ ८४ ॥

tato'gni-vacanāt sītāṁ jñātvā vigata-kalmaṣām |

karmaṇā tena mahatā trailokyaṁ sa-carācaram || 83 ||

sa-devarṣi-gaṇaṁ tuṣṭaṁ rāghavasya mahātmanaḥ |

babhau rāmaḥ samprahṛṣṭaḥ pūjitaḥ sarva-daivataiḥ || 84 ||

tataḥ– (ind.) then; **agni**– (m. n.) fire; **vacana**– (neu. n.) speech; **agni-vacanāt**– (tp. cp. neu. abl. sg.) due to the words of fire; **sītām**– (f. n. acc. sg.) Sītā; **jñātvā**– (abs., √jñā) having known; **vigata**– (ppp.) free from; **kalmaṣa**– (neu. n.) sin; **vigata-kalmaṣām**– (bv. cp./f. adj. acc. sg.) devoid of sins; **karmaṇā**– (neu. n. inst. sg.) by the deed; **tena**– (d. pron. neu. inst. sg.) by that; **mahatā**– (neu. adj. inst. sg.) great; **trailokyam**– (neu. n. nom. sg.) the three worlds[48]; **sa**– (ind.) with; **cara**– (adj.) moving; **acara**– (adj.) non-moving; **sa-carācaram**– (bv. cp./neu. adj. nom. sg.) with all moving and non-moving beings; **sa**– (ind.) with; **deva**– (m. n.) demigod; **ṛṣi**– (m. n.) sage; **gaṇa**– (m. n.) host; **sa-devarṣi-gaṇam**– (bv. cp./neu. adj. nom. sg.) with the hosts of sages and demigods; **tuṣṭam**– (ppp./neu. adj. nom. sg.) satisfied; **rāghavasya**– (m. n. gen. sg.) of Śrī Rāma; **mahat**– (adj.) great; **ātman**– (m. n.) soul; **mahātmanaḥ**– (bv. cp./m. adj. gen. sg.) great soul; **babhau**– (√ bhā, 3rd p. perf. sg.) looked splendid; **rāmaḥ**– (m. n. nom. sg.) Śrī Rāma; **samprahṛṣṭaḥ**– (ppp./m. adj. nom. sg.) joyful; **pūjitaḥ**– (ppp. m. nom. sg.) worshipped; **sarva**– (adj. pron.) all; **daivata**– (neu. n.) demigod; **sarva-daivataiḥ**– (tp. cp. m. inst. pl.) by all demigods.

---

[48] Lower, middle and upper (*bhūḥ, bhuvaḥ* and *svaḥ*).

Prose order

tataḥ agni-vacanāt sītāṁ vigata-kalmaṣāṁ jñātvā mahātmanaḥ rāghavasya tena mahatā karmaṇā sa-carācaraṁ sa-devarṣi-gaṇaṁ trailokyaṁ tuṣṭam | sarva-daivataiḥ pūjitaḥ rāmaḥ samprahṛṣṭaḥ babhau |

Translation

On account of the words of the fire god, all the three worlds, including the hosts of demigods, sages and all moving and non-moving beings who knew that Sītā was sinless, became satisfied with the great deed of the high-souled Rāma. Being worshipped by all the demigods, Śrī Rāma was joyful and looked splendid.

अग्निदेव के वचन से सीता को निष्पाप समझकर, महात्मा श्री राम के उस महान कर्म से देवता गण, ऋषि गण आदि त्रिभुवन के चराचर प्राणी संतुष्ट हो गए। देवताओं से पूजित होकर श्री राम प्रसन्न और सुशोभित हो गए।

TEXT 85

अभिषिच्य च लङ्कायां राक्षसेन्द्रं विभीषणम् ।

कृतकृत्यस्तदा रामो विज्वरः प्रमुमोद ह ॥ ८५ ॥

abhiṣicya ca laṅkāyāṁ rākṣasendraṁ vibhīṣaṇam |

kṛta-kṛtyas tadā rāmo vijvaraḥ pramumoda ha || 85 ||

abhiṣicya– (abs., abhi + √ sic) having consecrated; **ca**– (ind.) and; **laṅkāyām**– (f. n. loc. sg.) in Laṅkā; **rākṣasa**– (m. n.) demon; **indra**– (m. n.) king; **rākṣasendram**– (tp. cp. m. acc. sg.) king of the rākṣasas; **vibhīṣaṇam**– (m. n. acc. sg.) Vibhīṣaṇa[49]; **kṛta**– (ppp.) done; **kṛtya**– (neu. n.) duty; **kṛta-kṛtyaḥ**– (bv. cp./m. adj. nom. sg.) he who has performed his duties; **tadā**– (ind.) then; **rāmaḥ**– (m. n. nom. sg.) Śrī Rāma; **vijvaraḥ**– (m. adj. nom. sg.) devoid of anxiety; **pramumoda**– (pra + √ mud, perf. 3rd p. sg.) rejoiced; **ha**– (ind.) indeed.

Prose order

laṅkāyāṁ rākṣasendraṁ vibhīṣaṇam abhiṣicya tadā kṛta-kṛtyaḥ vijvaraḥ ca rāmaḥ pramumoda ha |

Translation

After consecrating Vibhīṣaṇa as the King of the rākṣasas in Laṅkā, Śrī Rāma finished His duties and rejoiced free from anxiety.

लंका में राक्षसराज के रूप में विभीषण का राज्याभिषेक करके श्री राम कृतार्थ और निश्चिन्त होकर आनंदित हो गए।

TEXT 86

देवताभ्यो वरं प्राप्य समुत्थाप्य च वानरान् ।

---

49 Rāvaṇa's brother.

अयोध्यां प्रस्थितो रामः पुष्पकेण सुहृद्वृतः ॥ ८६ ॥

devatābhyo varaṁ prāpya samutthāpya ca vānarān |

ayodhyāṁ prasthito rāmaḥ puṣpakeṇa suhṛd-vṛtaḥ || 86 ||

devatābhyaḥ– (f. n. abl. pl.) from the demigods; **varam**– (m. n. acc. sg.) blessings; **prāpya**– (abs., pra + √ āp) having obtained; **samutthāpya**– (abs., sam + ut + √ sthā) having made them rise from death; **ca**– (ind.) also; **vānarān**– (m. n. acc. pl.) monkeys; **ayodhyām**– (f. n. acc. sg.) to Ayodhyā; **prasthitaḥ**– (ppp. m. nom. sg.) departed; **rāmaḥ**– (m. n. nom. sg.) Śrī Rāma; **puṣpakeṇa**– (neu. n. inst. sg.) by an airplane made of flowers; **suhṛt**– (m. n.) friend; **vṛta**– (ppp.) surrounded; **suhṛd-vṛtaḥ**– (tp. cp./m. adj. nom. sg.) surrounded by friends.

Prose order

devatābhyaḥ varaṁ prāpya vānarān samutthāpya ca suhṛd-vṛtaḥ rāmaḥ puṣpakeṇa ayodhyāṁ prasthitaḥ |

Translation

Having received blessings from the demigods and having brought back to life the monkeys that had died in the battle, surrounded by friends Śrī Rāma departed for Ayodhyā in an airplane made of flowers.

देवताओं से वर लेकर और मारे गए बंदरों को पुनर्जीवित करके श्री राम ने अपने मित्रों के साथ पुष्पक विमान से अयोध्या की ओर प्रस्थान किया।

TEXT 87

भरद्वाजाश्रमं गत्वा रामः सत्यपराक्रमः ।

भरतस्यान्तिके रामो हनुमन्तं व्यसर्जयत् ॥ ८७ ॥

bharadvājāśramaṁ gatvā rāmaḥ satya-parākramaḥ |

bharatasyāntike rāmo hanumantaṁ vyasarjayat || 87 ||

bharadvāja– (m. n.) the sage Bharadvāja; **āśrama–** (neu. n.) hermitage; **bharadvājāśramam–** (tp. cp. neu. acc. sg.) the hermitage of the sage Bharadvāja; **gatvā–** (abs., √ gam) having gone; **rāmaḥ–** (m. n. nom. sg.) Śrī Rāma; **satya–** (adj.) real; **parākrama–** (m. n.) prowess; **satya-parākramaḥ–** (bv. cp./m. adj. nom. sg.) he whose prowess is real; **bharatasya–** (m. n. gen. sg.) of Bharata; **antike–** (ind./neu. n. loc. sg.) in the presence; **rāmaḥ–** (m. n. nom. sg.) Śrī Rāma; **hanumantam–** (m. n. acc. sg.) Hanumān; **vyasarjayat–** (vi + sarjay[50], imp. 3rd p. sg.) sent.

Prose order

satya-parākramaḥ rāmaḥ bharadvājāśramaṁ gatvā bharatasya antike hanumantaṁ vyasarjayat |

Translation

Approaching the hermitage of the sage Bharadvāja, Śrī Rāma, Who is truly heroic, sent Hanumān to Bharata.

---

[50] This is the causative verbal form of the root *sṛj.*

भरद्वाज मुनि के आश्रम पर जाकर सत्यपराक्रमी राम ने हनुमान को भरत के पास भेजा।

TEXT 88

पुनराख्यायिकां जल्पन् सुग्रीवसहितस्तदा ।

पुष्पकं तत् समारुह्य नन्दिग्रामं ययौ तदा ॥ ८८ ॥

punar ākhyāyikāṁ jalpan sugrīva-sahitas tadā |

puṣpakaṁ tat samāruhya nandigrāmaṁ yayau tadā || 88 ||

punaḥ– (ind.) again; **ākhyāyikām**– (f. n. acc. sg.) narrative; **jalpan**– (√ jalp, m. prp. nom. sg.) talking; **sugrīva**– (m. n.) Sugrīva; **sahita**– (adj.) together with; **sugrīva-sahitaḥ**– (tp. cp./m. adj. nom. sg.) together with Sugrīva; **tadā**– (ind.) then; **puṣpakam**– (neu. n. acc. sg.) the airplane made of flowers; **tat**– (d. pron. neu. acc. sg.) that; **samāruhya**– (sam + ā + √ ruh) having ascended; **nandigrāmam**– (m. n. acc. sg.) to Nandigrāma; **yayau**– (√ yā, perf. 3rd p. sg.) went; **tadā**– (ind.) then.

Prose order

tadā sugrīva-sahitaḥ tat puṣpakaṁ punaḥ samāruhya ākhyāyikāṁ jalpan tadā nandigrāmaṁ yayau |

Translation

Then, ascending again to the airplane made of flowers, Śrī Rāma departed for Nandigrāma while discussing with Sugrīva about the occurred incidents.

तब फिर से पुष्पक विमान पर आरूढ़ होकर श्री राम सुग्रीव के साथ बीती हुई घटनाओं के बारे में चर्चा करते हुए नंदिग्राम चले।

TEXT 89

नन्दिग्रामे जटां हित्वा भ्रातृभिः सहितोऽनघः ।

रामः सीतामनुप्राप्य राज्यं पुनरवाप्तवान् ॥ ८९ ॥

nandigrāme jaṭāṁ hitvā bhrātṛbhiḥ sahito'naghaḥ |

rāmaḥ sītām anuprāpya rājyaṁ punar avāptavān || 89 ||

nandigrāme– (m. n. loc. sg.) at Nandigrāma; **jaṭām**– (f. n. acc. sg.) matted locks of hair; **hitvā**– (abs., hā) having removed; **bhrātṛbhiḥ**– (m. n. inst. pl.) with His brothers; **sahitaḥ**– (m. adj. nom. sg.) together; **anaghaḥ**– (m. adj. nom. sg.) sinless; **rāmaḥ**– (m. n. nom. sg.) Śrī Rāma; **sītām**– (f. n. acc. sg.) Sītā; **anuprāpya**– (abs., anu + pra +√ āp) having gotten back; **rājyam**– (neu. n. acc. sg.) the kingdom; **punaḥ**– (ind.) again; **avāptavān**– (ava + √ āp, m. app. nom. sg.) reached.

Prose order

sītām anuprāpya nandigrāme jaṭāṁ hitvā bhrātṛbhiḥ sahitaḥ anaghaḥ rāmaḥ punaḥ rājyam avāptavān |

Translation

Having recovered Sītā, sinless Rāma removed His matted locks of hair in Nandigrāma and being accompanied by His brothers, He once again reached the Kingdom of Ayodhyā.

इस प्रकार सीता जी को फिर प्राप्त करके निष्पाप श्री राम नंदिग्राम में अपनी जटा त्याग कर अपने भाइयों के साथ फिर अयोध्या राज्य में पहुँचे।

Uttara-kāṇḍa

TEXT 90

प्रहृष्टमुदितो लोकस्तुष्टः पुष्टः सुधार्मिकः ।

निरामयो ह्यरोगश्च दुर्भिक्षभयवर्जितः ॥ ९० ॥

prahṛṣṭa-mudito lokas tuṣṭaḥ puṣṭaḥ su-dhārmikaḥ |

nirāmayo hy arogaś ca durbhikṣa-bhaya-varjitaḥ || 90 ||

prahṛṣṭa– (ppp./adj.) very delighted; **mudita**– (ppp./adj.) joyful; **prahṛṣṭa-muditaḥ**– (tp. cp./m. adj. nom. sg.) very delighted and joyful; **lokaḥ**– (m. n. nom. sg.) the people; **tuṣṭaḥ**– (m. adj. nom. sg.) satisfied; **puṣṭaḥ**– (m. adj. nom. sg.) nourished; **su**– (ind./pref.) well; **dhārmika**– (adj.) pious; **su-dhārmikaḥ**– (bv. cp./m. adj. nom. sg.) very pious; **nis**– (ind./pref.) without; **āmaya**– (m. n.) disease; **nirāmayaḥ**– (bv. cp./m. adj. nom. sg.) free from mental diseases; **hi**– (ind.) indeed; **a**– (ind./pref.) not; **roga**– (m. n.) sickness; **arogaḥ**– (bv. cp./m. adj. nom. sg.) without bodily sickness; **ca**– (ind.) and; **dus**– (ind./pref.) difficult; **bhikṣā**– (f. n.) begging; **dur-bhikṣa**– (tp. cp. neu. n.) famine; **bhaya**– (neu. n.) fear; **varjita**– (ppp.) devoid of; **durbhikṣa-bhaya-varjitaḥ**– (tp. cp./m. adj. nom. sg.) free from famine and fear.

Prose order

prahṛṣṭa-muditaḥ tuṣṭaḥ puṣṭaḥ su-dhārmikaḥ nirāmayaḥ hi arogaḥ durbhikṣa-bhaya-varjitaḥ ca lokaḥ |

Translation

Under Śrī Rāma's rule, the people will be exceedingly joyful, glad, satisfied, nourished, pious, devoid of mental and bodily ailments, and free from famine and fear.

श्री राम के शासन में प्रजा अत्यधिक प्रसन्न, सुखी, संतुष्ट, धार्मिक, मानसिक तथा शारीरिक रोगों से रहित और दुर्भिक्ष तथा भय से मुक्त होगी।

TEXT 91

न पुत्रमरणं केचिद् द्रक्ष्यन्ति पुरुषाः क्वचित् ।

नार्यश्चाविधवा नित्यं भविष्यन्ति पतिव्रताः ॥ ९१ ॥

na putra-maraṇaṁ kecid drakṣyanti puruṣāḥ kvacit |

nāryaś cāvidhavā nityaṁ bhaviṣyanti pati-vratāḥ || 91 ||

na– (ind.) not; **putra**– (m. n.) son; **maraṇa**– (neu. n.) death; **putra-maraṇam**– (tp. cp. neu. acc. sg.) death of a son; **kecit**– (indef. pron. m. nom. pl.) any; **drakṣyanti**[51]– (√ dṛś, fut. 3rd p. pl.) will see; **puruṣāḥ**– (m. n. nom. pl.) men; **kvacit**– (ind.) ever; **nāryaḥ**– (f. n. nom. pl.) women; **ca**– (ind.) and; **a**– (ind./pref.) not; **vi**– (ind./pref.) deprived of; **dhava**– (m. n.) husband; **vidhavā**– (f. n.) widow; **avidhavāḥ**– (bv. cp./f. adj. nom. pl.) not widowed; **nityam**– (ind.) always; **bhaviṣyanti**– (√ bhū, fut. 3rd p. pl.) will be; **pati**– (m. n.) husband; **vrata**– (n. n.) vow; **pati-vratāḥ**– (bv. cp./f. adj. nom. pl.) devoted to their husbands.

Prose order

na kecit puruṣāḥ putra-maraṇaṁ kvacit drakṣyanti nāryaḥ ca avidhavāḥ nityaṁ pati-vratāḥ bhaviṣyanti |

---

[51] From this verse there is a clear change from past to future tense. It is thus understood that Nārada Muni's meeting with Vālmīki took place some time after Śrī Rāma returned to Ayodhyā.

Translation

Men will never see the death of their sons. Women will be always devoted to their husbands and will never become widowed.

पुरुष अपने पुत्रों की मृत्यु कभी नहीं देखेंगे। नारियाँ हमेशा पतिव्रता होंगी और विधवा कभी नहीं होंगी।

TEXTS 92 - 93

न चाग्निजं भयं किञ्चिन्नाप्सु मज्जन्ति जन्तवः ।

न वातजं भयं किञ्चिन्नापि ज्वरकृतं तथा ॥ ९२ ॥

न चापि क्षुद्भयं तत्र न तस्करभयं तथा ।

नगराणि राष्ट्राणि च धनधान्ययुतानि च ॥ ९३ ॥

नित्यं प्रमुदिताः सर्वे यथा कृतयुगे तथा ।

na cāgni-jaṁ bhayaṁ kiñcin nāpsu majjanti jantavaḥ |

na vāta-jaṁ bhayaṁ kiñcin nāpi jvara-kṛtaṁ tathā || 92 ||

na cāpi kṣud-bhayaṁ tatra na taskara-bhayaṁ tathā |

nagarāṇi rāṣṭrāṇi ca dhana-dhānya-yutāni ca || 93 ||

nityaṁ pramuditāḥ sarve yathā kṛta-yuge tathā |

na– (ind.) not; **ca**– (ind.) and; **agni**– (m. n.) fire; **ja**– (adj.) born; **agni-jam**– (neu. adj. nom. sg.) produced by fire; **bhayam**– (neu. n. nom. sg.) fear; **kiñcit**– (indef. pron. neu. nom. sg.) any; **na**– (ind.) and; **apsu**– (f. n. loc. pl.) in the waters; **majjanti**– (√ majj, pr. 3rd p. pl.) drown; **jantavaḥ**– (m. n. nom. pl.) living beings; **na**– (ind.) not; **vāta**– (m. n.) wind; **ja**– (adj.) born; **vāta-jam**– (neu. adj. nom. sg.) produced by the wind; **bhayam**– (neu. n. nom. sg.) fear; **kiñcit**– (indef. pron. neu. nom. sg.) any; **na**– (ind.) and; **api**– (ind.) even; **jvara**– (m. n.) fever; **kṛta**– (ppp.) done; **jvara-kṛtam**– (tp. cp./neu. adj. nom. sg.) produced by fever; **tathā**– (ind.) as well; **na**– (ind.) not; **ca**– (ind.) and; **api**– (ind.) even; **kṣudh**– (f. n.) hunger; **bhayam**– (neu. n.) fear; **kṣud-bhayam**– (tp. cp. neu. nom. sg.) fear from starvation; **tatra**– (ind.) there; **na**– (ind.) not; **taskara**– (m. n.) thief; **bhaya**– (neu. n.) fear; **taskara-bhayam**– (tp. cp. neu. nom. sg.) fear from thieves; **tathā**– (ind.) as well; **nagarāṇi**– (neu. n. nom. pl.) towns; **rāṣṭrāṇi**– (neu. n. nom. pl.) territories; **ca**– (ind.) and; **dhana**– (neu. n.) wealth; **dhānya**– (neu. n.) grain; **yuta**– (adj.) filled with ; **dhana-dhānya-yutāni**– (tp. cp. neu. nom. pl.) filled with wealth and grains; **ca**– (ind.) and; **nityam**– (ind.) always; **pramuditāḥ**– (ppp./m. adj. nom. pl.) joyful; **sarve**– (adj. pron. m. nom. pl.) all; **yathā**– (ind.) just as; **kṛta-yuge**– (m. n. loc. sg.) in the Golden Age; **tathā**– (ind.) similarly.

Prose order

na ca agni-jaṁ kiñcit bhayaṁ na apsu jantavaḥ majjanti na vāta-jaṁ kiñcit bhayaṁ na api jvara-kṛtaṁ tathā na ca api kṣud-bhayaṁ tatra na taskara-bhayaṁ tathā | nagarāṇi ca rāṣṭrāṇi ca dhana-dhānya-yutāni | yathā kṛta-yuge tathā nityaṁ sarve pramuditāḥ |

Translation

In Śrī Rāma's kingdom, the towns and districts will be replete with wealth and grains. People will be as joyful as in Satya-yuga and there will be no fear of fire, wind, fever, hunger, and thieves at all. No living being will drown.

श्री राम के राज्य में सारे नगर और जिले धन तथा धान्य से भरे होंगे। लोग सत्य युग की भांति प्रसन्न होंगे। अग्नि, वायु, ज्वर, क्षुधा और चोरों से कुछ भी भय नहीं होगा। किसी भी प्राणी की पानी में डूबकर मृत्यु नहीं होगी।

TEXTS 94 - 96

अश्वमेधशतैरिष्ट्वा तथा बहुसुवर्णकैः ॥ ९४ ॥

गवां कोट्ययुतं दत्त्वा विद्वद्भ्यो विधिपूर्वकम् ।

असंख्येयं धनं दत्त्वा ब्राह्मणेभ्यो महायशाः ॥ ९५ ॥

राजवंशाञ् छतगुणान् स्थापयिष्यति राघवः ।

चातुर्वर्ण्यं च लोकेऽस्मिन् स्वे स्वे धर्मे नियोक्ष्यति ॥ ९६ ॥

aśvamedha-śatair iṣṭvā tathā bahu-suvarṇakaiḥ || 94 ||

gavāṁ koṭy-ayutaṁ dattvā vidvadbhyo vidhi-pūrvakam |

asaṁkhyeyaṁ dhanaṁ dattvā brāhmaṇebhyo mahā-yaśāḥ||95||

rāja-vaṁśāñ chata-guṇān sthāpayiṣyati rāghavaḥ |

cāturvarṇyaṁ ca loke'smin sve sve dharme niyokṣyati ||96||

aśva– (m. n.) horse; **medha**– (m. n.) sacrifice; **śata**– (num.) one hundred; **aśvamedha-śataiḥ**– (tp. cp. neu. inst. pl.) with one hundred horse sacrifices; **iṣṭvā**– (abs.,√ yaj) having sacrificed; **tathā**– (ind.) as well; **bahu**– (adj.) much; **suvarṇaka**– (neu. n.) gold; **bahu-suvarṇakaiḥ**– (tp. cp. neu. inst. pl.) with lots of gold[52]; **gavām**– (f. n. gen. pl.) of cows; **koṭi**– (f. n.) ten million; **ayuta**– (neu. n.) ten thousand; **koṭy-ayutam**– (dva. cp./neu. nom. sg.) ten million and ten thousand; **dattvā**– (abs., √ dā) having given; **vidvadbhyaḥ**– (m. n. dat. pl.) to the learned; **vidhi**– (m. n.) rule; **pūrva**– (adj.) accompanied by; **vidhi-pūrvakam**– (tp. cp. neu. nom. sg.) according to the rules; **asaṁkhyeyam**– (neu. adj. acc. sg.) uncountable; **dhanam**– (neu. n. acc. sg.) wealth; **dattvā**– (abs., √ dā) having given; **brāhmaṇebhyaḥ**– (m. n. dat. pl.) to the brāhmaṇas; **mahat**– (adj.) great; **yaśas**– (neu. n.) fame; **mahā-yaśāḥ**– (bv. cp./m. adj. nom. sg.) he whose fame is great; **rājan**– (m. n.) king; **vaṁśa**– (m. n.) dynasty; **rāja-vaṁśān**– (tp. cp./m. n. acc. pl.) the royal dynasties; **śata**– (num.) hundred; **guṇa**– (m. n.) virtue; **śata-guṇān**– (bv. cp./m. adj. acc. pl.) having hundreds of

52 The commentators Śiva Sahāya and Govindarāja explain *bahu-suvarṇaka* as a particular kind of sacrifice.

virtues; **sthāpayiṣyati**– (√ sthā, fut. 3rd p. sg.) will establish; **rāghavaḥ**– (m. n. nom. sg.) Śrī Rāma; **cāturvarṇyam**– (neu. n. acc. sg.) the four social orders; **ca**– (ind.) and; **loke**– (m. n. loc. sg.) in the world; **asmin**– (d. pron. m. loc. sg.) in this; **sve sve**– (pron. m. loc. sg.) own; **dharme**– (m. n. loc. sg.) duty; **niyokṣyati**– (ni + √ yuj, fut. 3rd p. sg.) will engage.

Prose order

mahā-yaśāḥ rāghavaḥ bahu-suvarṇakaiḥ aśvamedha-śataiḥ iṣṭvā tathā vidvadbhyaḥ gavāṁ koṭy-ayutaṁ vidhi-pūrvakaṁ dattvā brāhmaṇebhyaḥ asaṁkhyeyaṁ dhanaṁ dattvā śata-guṇān rāja-vaṁśān sthāpayiṣyati | asmin loke sve sve dharme cāturvarṇyaṁ niyokṣyati ca |

Translation

The glorious King Rāma will perform one hundred horse sacrifices with large quantities of gold and will give away millions of cows to the learned and unlimited wealth to the brāhmaṇas according to the scriptural rules. He will establish virtuous royal dynasties in the world and engage the four social orders in their respective duties.

महायशस्वी महाराज राम बहुत स्वर्ण युक्त एक सौ अश्वमेध यज्ञ करेंगे, विधिपूर्वक विद्वानों को कोटि कोटि गायें देंगे तथा ब्राह्मणों को असीमित धन देंगे। वे इस लोक में बहुत गुणी राजवंशों को स्थापित करेंगे और चारों वर्णों को अपने अपने धर्म में नियुक्त करेंगे।

TEXT 97

दशवर्षसहस्राणि दशवर्षशतानि च ।

रामो राज्यमुपासित्वा ब्रह्मलोकं प्रयास्यति ॥ ९७ ॥

daśa-varṣa-sahasrāṇi daśa-varṣa-śatāni ca |

rāmo rājyam upāsitvā brahma-lokaṁ prayāsyati || 97 ||

daśa– (num.) ten; **varṣa**– (neu. n.) year; **sahasra**– (num.) thousand; **daśa-varṣa-sahasrāṇi**– (tp. cp. neu. acc. pl.) ten thousand years; **daśa**– (num.) ten; **varṣa**– (neu. n.) year; **śata**– (num.) hundred; **daśa-varṣa-śatāni**– (tp. cp. neu. acc. pl.) ten times hundred years; **ca**– (ind.) and; **rāmaḥ**– (m. n. nom. sg.) Śrī Rāma; **rājyam**– (neu. n. acc. sg.) the kingdom; **upāsitvā**[53]– (abs., upa + √ ās) having ruled; **brahma**– (neu. n.) the Supreme Spirit; **loka**– (m. n.) world; **brahma-lokam**– (tp. cp./m. n. acc. sg.) the spiritual world; **prayāsyati**– (pra + √ yā, fut. 3rd p. sg.) will go.

Prose order

rāmaḥ daśa-varṣa-sahasrāṇi daśa-varṣa-śatāni ca rājyam upāsitvā brahma-lokaṁ prayāsyati |

Translation

Having ruled the kingdom for eleven thousand years, Śrī Rāma will go to the spiritual world.

---

[53] This is an irregular form instead of *upāsya.*

श्री राम ग्यारह हजार वर्ष तक राज्य शासन करके वैकुण्ठ लोक जाएँगे।

TEXT 98

इदं पवित्रं पापघ्नं पुण्यं वेदैश्च सम्मितम् ।

यः पठेद्रामचरितं सर्वपापैः प्रमुच्यते ॥ ९८ ॥

idaṁ pavitraṁ pāpa-ghnaṁ puṇyaṁ vedaiś ca sammitam |

yaḥ paṭhed rāma-caritaṁ sarva-pāpaiḥ pramucyate || 98 ||

idam– (d. pron. neu. acc. sg.) this; **pavitram**– (neu. adj. acc. sg.) pure; **pāpa**– (neu. n.) sin; **ghna**– (adj.) destroying; **pāpa-ghnam**– (tp. cp./neu. adj. acc. sg.) destroyer of sins; **puṇyam**– (neu. adj. acc. sg.) pious; **vedaiḥ**– (m. n. inst. pl.) with the Vedas; **ca**– (ind.) and; **sammitam**– (neu. adj. acc. sg.) similar to; **yaḥ**– (r. pron. m. nom. sg.) he who; **paṭhet**– (√ paṭh, opt. 3rd p. sg.) would read; **rāma**– (m. n.) Śrī Rāma; **carita**– (neu. n.) activity; **rāma-caritam**– (tp. cp. neu. acc. sg.) Śrī Rāma's activities; **sarva**– (adj. pron.) all; **pāpa**– (neu. n.) sin; **sarva-pāpaiḥ**– (tp. cp. neu. inst. pl.) from all sins; **pramucyate**– (pra + √ muc, pr. ps. 3rd p. sg.) is liberated.

Prose order

yaḥ pavitraṁ pāpa-ghnaṁ puṇyaṁ vedaiḥ ca sammitam idaṁ rāma-caritaṁ paṭhet sarva-pāpaiḥ pramucyate |

Translation

One who reads this narration of Śrī Rāma's activities, which is pure, pious, similar to the Vedas and destroys sins, will be free from all sins.

जो मनुष्य श्री राम के इस पवित्र, पापनाशक, पुण्यमय और वेदतुल्य चरित का अध्ययन करेगा, वह सब पापों से मुक्त हो जाएगा।

TEXT 99

एतदाख्यानमायुष्यं पठन् रामायणं नरः ।

सपुत्रपौत्रः सगणः प्रेत्य स्वर्गे महीयते ॥ ९९ ॥

etad ākhyānam āyuṣyaṁ paṭhan rāmāyaṇaṁ naraḥ |

sa-putra-pautraḥ sa-gaṇaḥ pretya svarge mahīyate || 99 ||

etat– (d. pron. neu. acc. sg.) this; **ākhyānam**– (neu. n. acc. sg.) narration; **āyuṣyam**– (neu. adj. acc. sg.) giving longevity; **paṭhan**– (√ paṭh, m. prp. m. sg.) reading; **rāmāyaṇam**– (neu. n. acc. sg.) named Rāmāyaṇa; **naraḥ**– (m. n. nom. sg.) a man; **sa**– (ind./pref.) together with; **putra**– (m. n.) son; **pautra**– (m. n.) grandson; **sa-putra-pautraḥ**– (bv. cp./m. adj. nom. sg.) accompanied by his sons and grandsons; **sa**– (ind./pref.) together with; **gaṇa**– (m. n.) associates; **sa-gaṇaḥ**– (bv. cp./m. adj. nom. sg.) with his associates; **pretya**– (abs., pra + √ ī) having passed away; **svarge**–

(m. n. loc. sg.) in heaven; **mahīyate**– (√mahī, pr. 3rd p. sg.) becomes exalted.

Prose order

etat āyuṣyaṁ rāmāyaṇam ākhyānam paṭhan naraḥ sa-putra-pautraḥ sa-gaṇaḥ pretya svarge mahīyate |

Translation

This narration of the Rāmāyaṇa yields longevity and by reading it one will be exalted in heaven after death, accompanied by sons, grandsons and associates.

यह रामायण कथा आयुष वर्धक है और इसका अध्ययन करते हुए मनुष्य देहांत के बाद अपने पुत्र, पौत्र और परिजन के साथ स्वर्ग में महान होगा।

TEXT 100

पठन् द्विजो वागृषभत्वमीयात्

स्यात् क्षत्रियो भूमिपतित्वमीयात् ।

वणिग् जनः पण्यफलत्वमीयाज्

जनश्च शूद्रोऽपि महत्त्वमीयात् ॥ १०० ॥

paṭhan dvijo vāg-ṛṣabhatvam īyāt

syāt kṣatriyo bhūmi-patitvam īyāt |

vaṇig janaḥ paṇya-phalatvam īyāj

janaś ca śūdro'pi mahattvam īyāt || 100 ||

paṭhan– (√ paṭh, m. prp. nom. sg.) reading; **dvijaḥ**– (m. n. nom. sg.) a brāhmaṇa; **vāk**– (f. n.) speech; **ṛṣabhatva**– (neu. n.) excellence; **vāg-ṛṣabhatvam**– (tp. cp. neu. acc. sg.) excellence in speech; **īyāt**– (√ i or √ ī, opt. 3rd p. sg.) attains; **syāt**– (√ as, opt. 3rd p. sg./ind.) would be/ if; **kṣatriyaḥ**– (m. n. nom. sg.) a kṣatriya; **bhūmi**– (f. n.) land; **patitva**– (neu. n.) lordship; **bhūmi-patitvam**– (tp. cp. neu. acc. sg.) lordship over land; **īyāt**– (√ i or √ ī, opt. 3rd p. sg.) attains; **vaṇik**– (m. n. nom. sg.) a vaiśya; **janaḥ**– (m. n. nom. sg.) a person; **paṇya**– (neu. n.) business; **phalatva**– (neu. n.) fruitfulness; **paṇya-phalatvam**– (tp. cp. neu. acc. sg.) fruitfulness in business; **īyāt**– (√ i or √ ī, opt. 3rd p. sg.) attains; **janaḥ**– (m. n. nom. sg.) a person; **ca**– (ind.) and; **śūdraḥ**– (m. n. nom. sg.) a śūdra; **api**– (ind.) even; **mahattvam**– (neu. n. acc. sg.) greatness; **īyāt**– (√ i or √ ī, opt. 3rd p. sg.) attains.

Prose order

paṭhan dvijaḥ vāg-ṛṣabhatvam īyāt syāt kṣatriyaḥ bhūmi-patitvam īyāt vaṇik janaḥ paṇya-phalatvam īyāt śūdraḥ janaḥ ca api mahattvam īyāt |

Translation

If one reading this Rāmāyaṇa is a brāhmaṇa, he attains excellence in speech; if a kṣatriya, he becomes the king of a land; if a vaiśya, he obtains success in business; and if a śūdra, he also becomes an important person.

यदि रामायण का अध्ययन करने वाला ब्राह्मण हो, तो वह वाक्पटु हो जाएगा; क्षत्रिय हो, तो राज्य प्राप्त करेगा; वैश्य व्यापार में सफलता प्राप्त करेगा; और शूद्र भी महान हो जाएगा।

|| śrī-śrī-sītā-rāma-tadīyārpaṇam astu ||

Made in the USA
Coppell, TX
04 September 2022

82613194R00075